Dearest Luminea

May your Path be
blessed always an
the lady walk a
by yourside.
my love & bless
clearest sister

Phiona Hutton
xxx

Book Cover Designed By Suzanne Southerton.
ISBN: 978-1-4466-1981-0

From the Whispers of Avalon

By
Phiona Hutton

Book Dedication

The Whispers of Avalon is dedicated to all those who are lost within the mist. Who hear the call of the Great Mother and Lady. For those who have searched for Avalon, she calls to you, she reaches through the mist and embraces you within her heart upon the gentle sigh of a whisper. I would like to thank all who have been within my life and helped me walk my path to Avalon. Who have stood with me through the tough times. Have bought me the lessons I have needed to learn. Who have loved me and nourished me. Who have helped me find forgiveness, passion and love. You all know who you are and I hold you lovingly within my heart.To my husband who graciously allows me often to wander the realm of Avalon, whenever I have the need, and to my three beautiful Children for whom without I simply would not be.

)O(

Forward

A Book of whispered words upon the winds from the Lady of
Avalon. Weaved through the mists to the realm of man. Calling the
souls of all those who have walked the path of the sacred Isle and
invoking memories and emotions that will lead you back home.
I am a seer, I have always been and will always be.

As I look into the dark blue pool of the oracle water of the sacred
Isle, I hear the whispers from the ancients and the wise, and those
who have walked this path before.
Now through the mists I bring them to you, to help you walk your
path. With clarity and strength, wisdom and support, truth and
integrity, and a knowing that you are never alone. For she of all
things walks forever by your side.

)O(

About the Author

I am a child of the old ways and a daughter of Avalon. I have always heard the Lady Priestess as she whispers her words to me and have shared the wisdom she brings with those around me for many years.

I used to talk to her as a child and just believed that everyone else could hear her too. It was only as I aged that I realised that she was talking to me and that she wanted me to share her words with the world.

I follow the path of the Priestess and of the craft and embrace the wisdom the Great Mother passes to me. Now through "From the Whispers of Avalon" I have placed her whispers together in a book from the Lady herself to share with you.

I have long walked the path of the ancients. Taking my guidance from the messages that nature holds. Embracing the gentle path of the Mother Goddess. Choosing to stand aside from the modern teaching of the world today.

I have lived through many lifetimes upon this beautiful planet, and my heart belongs to the Sacred Isle of Avalon. I am a priestess of Avalon, and follow her sacred lore. The teachings of the Great Mother and the Wise man.

As a priestess of Avalon I attune to the energies of the hidden ways, finding sanctuary within the moon and awakening to the rhythm of nature. I work with these energies within my healing as they bring a gentle clarity to the soul. Allowing folk to awaken, rebalance, heal and fully embrace their soul journey and path.

I have walked the path for many lifetimes and always been a daughter of the Goddess. The old ways walked by my side throughout my childhood and I always heard the whispers of the ancients. My family hails from Briton, Ireland and Scotland alike and I have strong Celtic blood flowing through my veins.

I was often visited by a woman in blue who would sit by my bed side stroking my hair. She would weep when I cried and she would embrace me when I felt alone. She whispered words into my ear and gave medreams of a beautiful isle where I would return when I was ready.
As I aged I realised she was the Lady of Avalon and she was watching her daughter of the Mists.

I have long worked with the realm of the Fae and since a child have communed with them. My oldest guide was a Fae I called Norman who was with me from very early childhood. He showed me the magic of the realm, and how to work alongside its energy within our own time and space. He showed me many things, how to hold energy and weave it into our world. As I grew up I realised his name was Dorrell and he hailed from the Merlin's of Avalon. He walks with me to this day. Now I guide and teach others to connect and open up to the realms of the Fae.

I have always had the gift of the Empath. The gift of the claircognizant. The energy of the healer. I was obsessed with the wise woman and witch as a child, not realizing that it was my past life recall that drew me.
I was often found within the garden talking with "my Friends " that

only I could see. Sending my wishes into the winds and often found them returned in the most mysterious ways.

My days were filled with horses and I craved the freedom they bought me. It still makes me cry to this day to touch a horse. They carried me when I had no strength to continue. They touched me with the energy of the unicorn and opened me to the realm from where they reside.

After a great trauma when I was eleven I turned inwards and away from the magical realms. Although they never left me I chose to walk my human path and through many lessons I became lost and heavy.

Then in my Twenties I knew there was a part of me lost. I went searching for her and found myself on a healing path. The voices I had always heard were becoming louder. I always knew things, I was always right.

The lady still with me guided me to find teachers and wise ones within this realm. I was initiated into a local traditional coven and worked through the degrees within them, becoming High Priestess. But it felt so empty.

I still knew there was more. I walked away from Wicca, and once I did so my memory became renewed. The Mists lifted the veil between this realm and Avalon was no longer out of reach I was home. I was within Avalon once more. The teachings, the whisper of the Lady upon the winds filling my head with her words.

I had found myself. I started teaching the Avalon ways, the ways of the ancient ones. Over the last 15 years I have grown into the Priestess I always was. The lady no longer weeps at my side. She stands by my side. Sharing the wisdom she holds with me, and I share it within the Whispers of Avalon.

I live with my husband and three children all of whom hail from the Fae. I work as a healer and teacher of the old ways. I have been called to connect the Sisters of the Mists for a while now, yet it is only now that it feel the right time to do so. Working the magic of Albion and the Celtic truths that are found behind the mists.

My greatest guide is that of the Unicorn. I have often been called " Her of the Unicorns". Their gentle energy and guidance helps us to open our hearts and heal within. I have long walked with a Unicorn by my side and treasure the gift that they hold. Pure of heart and pure of magic.

My journey within this lifetime is that of the teacher and healer, bringing Avalon back to her rightful place within this realm. I have undergone many personal lessons to become the soul I am today. I have often felt alone and have dealt with the lessons of abandonment, rejection and depression within my journey. It has enabled me to become the healer I am today and to guide folk into healing their lives. Looking at their past and embracing their journey upon this planet.
The Lady walks by my side and whispers to my soul. May she whisper to you also, embracing you to her core.

Many blessings to you

)O(

Contents

Whispers

of

Avalon

If I hold my Breath so very Still

If I hold my breath so very still, I am within Avalon at my will.
Surrounded by the Earth so green, this gentle place I have always seen.
Colours bright and sound so clear, the touch of the Fae so very near.
Within my fingertips a magical power, that grows within me with every hour.
Here I feel such a loving air, that no man or mortal can compare.
Beautiful priestess sits beside me, and holds my hand so tenderly.
She looks within me with her gift of sight, and before I know it day becomes night.
The sky is filled by the light of the fire, as my soul soars higher and higher.
The priestess energy rises within me , I am now all I can ever be.
My being is fulfilled by the energy pure, but within me there is a subtle lure.
Taking me home to the land of man, to teach all those who we can.
The teachings of the old, the ancient and wise, embracing the ancestors as they rise.
If I hold my breath so very still , I am within Avalon at my will.

)O(

The Sacred Energies

The Sacred energies are coming back to the land.
I feel the power growing within my hand.
The ancient mysteries are becoming clear.
The return of the Unicorns is coming near.
A time when all the realms become one.
The time of the Old Religion nearly begun.
The Dragons and Fae are returning now.
And to them I turn in honoured bow.
For Avalon now is shining through the myst's.
The call of the Great Mother I cannot resist.
All becoming one, and one becoming all.
I answer the song that my soul hears call.

)O(

Children Of Avalon

Children of Avalon it is time to rise, for I see the ancients within
your eyes.

Remember the rites we used to attend, with our mind and will time
we can bend.

To the ancient hour of the sacred place, through the mists I can
see the magical space.

Walk with me now daughter of old , the time is right to teach the
secrets we hold.

Raise her up to her rightful place, the Mother priestess full of
grace.

The sacred symbols are drawn upon me, as I embrace this
powerful & wise energy.

Within my soul is the knowledge of old, that embraces me within
the Priestess fold.

I will walk my path alone or with kin, but I walk the path holding the
truths within.

I hold my hand for those who seek, my promise to you I will always
keep.

To teach you all the ancient truths, that I have carried with me
since my youth.

The love of the Great mother is ours to share, If we open our
hearts if only we dare.

Avalon awaits for those who seek. The ancient secrets are ours to
keep.

Walk the path of the gentle Priestess, to lead a life that is truly
blessed.

One of balance and the magical lore, to rekindle the time that has
gone before.

The time is right and the time is now, as I recognise you with the humble bow.

Priestess come walk with me, as we become all I know we can be.

)O(

As the Silent boat nudges gently at the shore

As the silent boat nudges gently at the shore ,I am in my beloved
Avalon once more.
I step upon the grass so green, that only the ancients and wise
have seen.
Within the great circle are my sisters and kin, they open the
doorway to allow me in.
With our hands and faces raised to the sky, within this place I
cannot deny.
My spirit and soul sings so aloud, as I recognise my sisters within
the crowd.
From the great fire the images are seen, as we weave and create
the beautiful May Queen.
The Hunter is created with prowess and power, as he takes his
queen within this hour.
They disappear into the falling mist, to return at Beltane with the
lovers Kiss.
Created and called upon the April seed moon, the Great mother
blesses us with her precious boon.
The time has come to return to this world, and within the boat my
body is curled.
As I travel back through time and space, my heart holds a tear as I
leave this place.
For within this time I am recognised as one, the empowered
Priestess of Avalon.

)O(

I long to be in Avalon

I long to be in Avalon, I close my eyes and there I be.
Upon the boat I stand alone, within the mists and sea.
The silence that surrounds me is deafening in its power.
Time has no movement here not even by the hour.
The boat nudges softly at the green bank of grass.
Upon the gentle Mother Earth I now step at last.
The priestess welcomes me with arms open wide.
Within the magic circle I now step inside.
My magic and my power grows beyond belief.
To be among my sisters, my souls finds such relief.
I really think I will stay awhile, not to return to soon.
At least until the blessing of the April full moon.

)O(

My soul has many words to say

My soul has many words to say.
It speaks from the Isle of Avalon today.
An enchanted place full of magic and Fae.
Will you dare to tread your journey this way?
It will question your soul to the deepest parts.
It will find the truths within your heart.
Freedom can be found within this place.
Just open your mind to this sacred space.
It will bring treasures beyond your wildest dreams.
Clearly illuminated by silver moonbeams.
Take my hand if it's too much to face.
And allow me to guide you to the land of grace.

)O(

The Path to Avalon

The path before me opens, I see where I need to be.
Will you walk by my side and journey with me to the place of the
ancients?
As I walk the path I feel the stones underneath my feet, reminding
me of the paths I walked and that have lead me to today.
I follow this path of enlightenment and I hear the sounds of the
sacred chants before me.
My soul begins to rise as I welcome this sound within my being.
For it is the sound of the ancients, the time of Avalon and her
Priestess.
As I turn the corner I see my home, I see Avalon, my sisters,
my brethren.
Here the colours are so intense, the sounds are carried upon the
silent hush of nature.
The Great Mother is all around me, I am home.
I enter the great circle, symbols of our path are placed before me
to wear and embrace.
As I step from the realm of man, I become the Priestess once
more.
The Celtic breath grips me like the flow of Ice throughout my body
cleansing every part.
I no longer speak with the tongue of man, but that of the Priestess.
I become her, I breathe her, my heart beats the rhythm of her.
As she rises through my body I am consumed by her, my magic is
her, she is me, the Celtic Priestess of Avalon.
The energy rises and I am joined by my sisters, with tears filling
my eyes I am embraced within such beauty.
Within such magic, It pulses through my body, I become the seer
I become all that I know I am and more, I become free.

No more will I walk alongside this place, Avalon lives within my heart, my soul, my very being.
I will return to the realm of man, but not of man. I will walk as the Priestess for evermore, bringing the teachings of the Mother Goddess with me for those that seek to find the lessons they bring.

)O(

Beyond the path that meanders through the valley

Beyond the path that meanders through the valley, where the
highest hill can be seen for miles is an Isle they call Avalon.
Shrouded behind the veil of mist an enchanted land that awaits the
soul who seeks her.
But not for the weak of mind or for the delicate soul ,only those
who dare to tread, will do
battle with all that they know and open their soul to the Goddess.

She holds within her gentle breast the love of the Mother Goddess,
the wisdom of the universes, and the knowledge of all the times of
before.
The sacred books within their pages the words of the ancient and
wise, only to be read by
those who are embraced within the mists.

Here all is one, the unicorn with his majesty and pure power
walks among the two leggeds with honour and acceptance.
The Dragon safely embraced by those who know him, a usual
sight for the priestess as she walks the spiral of daily visualisation.
The Fae working alongside without fear or disbelief by those
around her. All is one.

Peace fills the air, harmony is all around, and tranquility is the
breath of life.
Power is the balance of all things, growth is abundant, no one
wants or needs for they just are.
Yet many choose to leave this sacred place, to walk through the
mists, to leave their beloved home as they travel through the veil
and to the realm of man.

They journey to bring the teachings and knowledge to those who

call for her, yet are too alone to take the path they need to tread.
To weak to find her, to afraid to embrace her, they gently find
these souls and hold their hand, helping them to their feet and
walking by their side.
They are the wayshowers, the guides of Avalon, seeking the
souls who left the lands long
ago to journey in the different realms, and lost the way home.
They will always find you, embrace and nurture you, for the
priestess is within us all.
The hunter within our soul, the sacred union in our hearts.
Avalon calls you, for she is rising. Returning to her height.
The Mother Goddess is awakening. The time of the mists is here.

)O(

Upon this path I have walked for miles

Upon this path I have walked for miles
Through many lessons I have learnt my craft
At my feet is always the Earth
Within my being the light of the stars.

From the Celtic path and of the Mother
To the lands of the Merlin and the Father
The hunter of the glorious hunt
And the Huntress of the harvest.

To breath within the gift of nature
Within the freedom of my soul
Is a blessing of the Mother Priestess
And an awakening of the essence of my being.

The Mother came to me in my dreams before my birth
She told me of my paths before
And of the Path I would walk this time
She promised to walk with me and always be at my side.

From the stirrings of the unfurled bud at the time of spring within
To the floating of the falling leaf at the autumn does begin
I follow the whisper of nature as she talks softly in my ear
To be a part of her journey with every breath I take.

I stand behind the mists within my chosen home
The place they call Avalon of the ancients and the olds

The place where I belong and find my hearts true beat
From the Whispers of Avalon my heart sings its loudest song

)O(

Within the heart of the ancient soul

Within the heart of the ancient soul, dwells wisdom and magic of a
forgotten time.
We search for the Isle that burns in our lives , with the light of the
Flame of Avalon.
Embers of the fire from within the veil, scattered across land and
time.
One day she will rise above the mists, bringing her children safely
home.

We are not the forgotten ones or the ones that time forgot.
We are the awakened souls of the Priestess and Priests of the
Elders time.
We have within our souls and hearts the energy and knowledge of
old.
Now is the time to free ourselves and step from the realm of man.

Stand before her children of the old ways, and honour her sacred
rites.
For now we see she of all things, within our eyes and mind.
Free her upon the breath of your words and within your daily
chore.
She of many names, but the Great Mother Goddess to all.

The sacred union between hunter and huntress dwells within our
loins.
We give birth to them within our lives and bring wisdom to one
and all.
As the mystic Isle rises up to be in her rightful place, Sister, brother

stand together now.
Hand to hand and eye to eye in the circle of the old's.

We listen as we stand of the tales that went before.
To bring them to the modern lands, the mysteries of the wise.
We hear the call of the Avalon crone and we honour and obey.
The Priestess of the sacred Isle, silently walks her path always.

The knowledge that she holds within, so pure of of high intent.
The power of the essence she holds within her hand.
To empower the elements and the realm of the forgotten lands.
Her time is now, to rise up through the mist, to be seen for
evermore.

No longer hidden in time, beyond the reach of the ones that cannot
see.
Free to walk the worlds of mystical beast and magical kingdoms.
To hold the Whispers of the ancient lore within her silent words.
To honour the ancients with every step and bring her teachings to
all.

)O(

Whispers of the Great Mother

Walk With Me

Walk with me daughter of old, as we step together you and I .
I will lead you to the seers pool who's waters reflect the sky.
Within it if you take a look holds that answers to all.
If your willing to to face your fears and honour the ancient call.

I am as old as time and holder of the sacred truths.
I walk this path along your side since the gentle days of your
youth.
I have always been and shall always be within the air you breath.
You only need to close your eyes and call my name to show me
you believe.

I am the essence within nature that births all our dreams.
Nothing I say or do is ever as it seems.
I am the Gentle mother whose path you chose to follow.
My journey is the one of joy, not regret or sorrow.

Do not look for me for you will never find me where you seek.
I am within the winds and the gentle winding creek.
I am the beauty of the rainstorm and the turbulent scudding
sky.
Within the growth of the flower and the tear-drop of the cry.

I will always be with you, truthful, honest and wise.
Whenever you need me, call my name into the skies.
Walk your path with honour, integrity and lore.
For you walk it with the ancients and those who went before.
)O(

Through the Time of Times

Through the times of time and time that man has forgot, holds the
ancient truths within the essence of my soul.
From Lemuria to Atlantis. From Egypt to the Aztec's and to my
beloved Avalon.
The energy of the universal truths empowered within magic.
We are all energy of the Divine Mother Goddess, all teachings of
the sacred lore.
Now hidden behind the mists, only revealed to those who hold the
ancient key within their soul.
The Priestess has long since dwelt away from the realm of man for
her truths are honoured by the Gods and often feared by man
himself.
Her ways are of the land and of nature, of the Elders and the wise.
She holds no weight to the rules and ways of those who reside
outside of the Veil of Avalon.
She walks among her sisters, where one respects the other, where
one and all are the same.
In honour of the old ways and the gentle love of the Great Mother.
Yet with a power that can unleash the wrath of the elements within
the palms of their hands.
The seer whose gift of sight is often unwanted within the realm of
man, for it can bring a fear of the unseen.
But for the priestess it brings connection and knowing that brings
balance to all things.
I choose to walk through the mists and hold the gateway for those
who seek.

To allow them to embrace the secret realms.

For we are not to be hidden within folklore, myth or tales. The time for us to awaken man and bring our gifts upon this place.

)O(

Of All the things I can not see

Of all the things I cannot see, I always know who I am to be.
The empowered child from a different time, a blessed place, with
the love of the Goddess within my face.
I know that I stand alone, when I connect with the energy of my
home.
So many around move without connection and at great race, I
wonder when they last felt the ancient pace.
My body beats to the beat of the drum, that draws us all to be one.
I hear the call loudly as it pulses throughout my being, and I feel
the energies rise without seeing.
Ancient Mother who birthed me here, how I long for you to be near.
I feel so out of my time and place, I yearn for the time of the sacred
Avalon space.

)O(

Where have you Been?

Where have you been daughter of mine? For you I cannot see or cannot find.

I have walked the path of the mystic lore and looked into the places you have dwelled before.

You seem to have gone from my sight, covered and shrouded by the darkness of night.

I cannot reach you when I call your name, when within an instant you always came.

Daughter of the fae your energy has all but slipped away.

Come to me now as I call. The ancient words whispered upon my breath.

Return to me hence, upon your path and rejoice within my mirth.

Daughter of the wise and sister of the ancestors rise once more.

)O(

She Took Me by the hand

She took me by the hand and I felt her heart give a gentle sigh.

Child of mine what is so wrong? As she stared lovingly into my

eyes.

You seem so lost within this world, come with me through the

myst.

To a place we call Avalon that no ancient soul can resist.

I trusted she who had no name but was known by all around.

For within her love I knew that this lost soul now was found.

Now from the path of the ancients this priestess does tread.

And only to the beat of the earth will my heart ever more be led.

)O(

She raises up from the Earth so green

She raises up from the Earth so green, gentle goddess the ancients have seen.

Great mother in her nurturing guise. She has laid here for eternity under the changing skies.

Here for you in a moments call. Here gentle arms catching you when you fall.

Gentle mother walk with me as I honour your beauty deep within me.

For I am the child of she who is all. In my soul deep is her ancient call.

)O(

She of the old ways

She of the old ways, of everything that was and everything to come.
She of the ancient path of magic and lore.
She of the silent folk of the fae and of the night.
She who holds the power of the elements within her hands.

The lady of the circle whose word is soft and true.
The lady of the cauldron whose power is intense.
The lady of the sight whose eye never tells a deceit.
The lady of the many who is equal among the men.

The priestess of the craft from the time of long ago.
The priestess of the new souls who guides along the path.
The priestess of the familiar who listens to the call.
The priestess of the Lord and lady who bows to their knowledge.

Who is she who walks this path? She lives within you and within me.
She is the divine ancient soul of the Great mother that runs though our veins.
She is the breath of the morning breeze. The whisper within the bird song.
The glowing sun upon your face. The warming fire within your hearth.

The gentle shower of the spring rain and the torrential rains of the fall.

She is the balance within us and around us. She is the truth within our hearts.

I will honour her with every breath and every step.

For to be without her is not to live at all.

)O(

Over the water I can see the haze

Over the water I can see the haze. It calls to me in a distant song.
As I open my sight seer gaze.
My gazing pool so deep and blue holds the answers deep
within.
I call for knowledge and wisdom true. What do I see today?. What
questions do you seek?
From the ancients and the Fae, for within this pool only the
ancients do speak,
Holders of the secrets and of the wisdom you do seek.
So come and sit a while and listen to the words of the messages
from the sacred Isle.

)O(

To the souls who have walked this path before

To the souls who have walked this path before.
To the ancients who told stories of what they saw.
To the wise women and to the cunning men.
Who worshipped the craft in a hidden glen.
To those who led us from the darkness to light.
And gave their lives in the cover of night.
To our brothers and sisters of the hidden lore.
Who were persecuted like never before.
To those who hid in fear of their life.
Father, mother, brother and wife.
Drowned and burned for their love of the Great mother.
For the honour and protection of one another.
We will never forget such horror you saw.
We will honour you her for ever more.

)O(

She whispers to me

She whispers to me through time and space. Lady of old and of the sacred place.
She knows my path and my journey so far, for she has walked with me under every star.
Lady of the mist and of the ancient ways, How I longed for you in my childhood days.
You called to me on the breath of the fae and Avalon I saw through their enchanting gaze.

My Lady, my mother, my teacher and my guide. You lifted the mists and allowed me inside.
Within my home I stood once more. With the knowing of here I had stood before.
Now I return in a moments hush. To the realm of man I never rush.
To stand within this sacred space within the circle my rightful place.

)O(

Whispers of the Priestess

To Be a Priestess

To be a Priestess is to find balance within all things.

To be a Priestess is to walk the path of our sisters alone.

To be a priestess is to hold the grace of nature within your soul.

To be a priestess is to honour the ancients and the wisdom they bring.

To be a Priestess is to honour your feelings and respect the outcome.

To be a priestess is to conjure the power of the elements.

To be a priestess is to be the keeper of secrets, yet the teacher to those who seek.

To be a priestess is to be open to the truths that at times bring loneliness and pain.

To be a priestess is to walk with the ancestors as they stand by our side daily.

To be a priestess is to be the holder of the keys that open many paths.

To be a priestess is to open the great gates of the other realms with respect.

To be a priestess is to be always open, growing and learning no matter how old.

To be a priestess is to hold the wisdom of the gifts of the Earth.

To be a priestess is to embrace the power within and so without.

To be a priestess is to blend the wisdom and Knowledge for the greater good.

To be a priestess is to not live in fear of the darker energies, but to harness them.

To be a priestess is to honour the plants and animals as a reflection of ourselves.

To be a priestess is to be silent in your wisdom, strength and power.

To be a priestess is to listen to the wisdom of the Moon and the clarity of the sun

To be a priestess is to walk the path within the realm of man, with the knowledge of who you are.

To be a priestess is to honour the old ways with integrity and valour.

To be a priestess is to be of the Gods and Goddesses.

To be a priestess is to hold the sacred truths within your soul.

To be a priestess is to always have the protection of the Great Mother at your feet.

To be a priestess is to step with the unicorn, dragon and Fae.

To be a priestess is to be.

)O(

To Stand Alone

To stand alone takes strength.
To be free takes strength beyond measure.
To follow your path when those around you chastise you for your
beliefs takes courage beyond the normal.

To be a priestess is to be free.
To be a priestess is to be strong.
To stand alone takes a belief in your power within and around you.
To follow the path of Avalon is to embrace the strength of the
Great Mother.

It is to run with the hunter.
It is to walk with the ancients with every step.
It is to look for the unseen.
It is to harness the energy of the elements, of the fae and of the
wise ones.

It is to open your path to learning and to being.
It is at times to walk within shadow.
To embrace the cold darkness of the lesson.
It is to walk with the herb lore within your heart.

It is to be at one with the
unicorn and dragon.
It is to be true to yourself.
It is to honour the divine within every living thing.

It is to be the healer and to be healed.

It is to embrace the mighty power and become it not to be the ego
of it.

It is hold the knowledge without compromise. It is to teach the
sacred truths to those that seek it.

It is to answer only to yourself and the Mother Goddess.

To walk the path of Avalon is to be truly free. For no man can bind
you. No man can hold you.

For you are bound to the magic of the sacred Isle.

You are the priestess if you choose
to be.

I am priestess. Avalon lives within every breath I take. Every
lesson I learn. Every moment that passes.

I am priestess.

)O(

In My Darkest days

In my darkest days, you always shine.
In my loneliest times I always have you.
In the times of great sadness you fill my heart.
In the times of fear you stand by my side.

When I am lost, you always find me.
When I am unseen you always see me.
When I am unheard you always here me.
When I am in doubt, you always centre me.

You are my breath, my life and my being.
Great Mother I honour you as I honour myself.
For we are of the same cloth the same essence of life.
Within my home of nature itself I am blessed beyond all realms.

I walk with integrity and with love within my soul.
With the joy and wonder of life within my heart.
My magic and power at the touch of my finger tips.
With the knowing within my very core.

I am priestess of the old ways.
I walk upon the path of the ancient lore.
I hold the whispers of the wise within my very being.
I honour the Elders within every aspect of my life.

Great Mother I call upon thee to walk with me today.
Allowing me to be all I can be.

To show me the steps I must take to become.

I am of the world of man yet from the realm of Avalon.

I will be true till the end of my journey as I teach those who ask.

I am priestess.

)O(

Gentle mother walk with me

Gentle Mother walk with me, show me all the things I know I can be.

Stand with me at my side the ever gentle loving guide.

Give me the strength to grow and flourish as from the earth I take food to nourish.

Herbs and flowers lovingly grown as from the hands of the Goddess they were sown.

Dreams and wishes weaved within. With the turn of the cycle they begin.

)O(

Avalon around me

Avalon around me.
Avalon within me.
Avalon I am.

Priestess awaken.
Priestess become.
Priestess I am.

All I have been.
All I am.
All I will ever be.

The seer of old.
The healer of the wise.
The enchantress of the ancients.

The daughter of the Goddess.
The sister of the Great Mother.
Child of the old ways.

I am priestess.
I am her.
I am me.

)O(

Silent Mother

Silent mother guide my feet as I walk my path today.

Gracious sister sit with me as I rest my soul a while.

Warrior father keep me safe as I journey through my life.

Sacred priestess walk with me as I step within the enchanted realm.

Great mother hear my words as I whisper into the night.

Gentle moon awash my spirit as the magic runs through my bones.

Ancestors stand by me as we connect the web of light.

Elders see me as the daughter of your knowledge.

Mother Avalon welcome me home as I step from the realm of man.

.

May I be blessed by the energies around me.

May the Goddess walk with you always.

)O(

I close my eyes and there you be

I close my eyes and there you be, the gracious Goddess who
always sees me.
I am not alone on my darkened days, For I see you there within my
gaze.
Gentle mother with your nurturing caress, within your words my
soul is blessed.
"Daughter of old what troubles you so?, within you are the
answers I know.
Listen to the rhythm of the ancient beat, as you tread your path
with uncovered feet.
They will take you to the sacred place, that makes your spirit soar
and your heartbeat race.
Don't wander too far as you follow your path, the journey you travel
to find your worth.
I walk by your side within every step, as you heal your past, your
emotions and regrets.
As your journey lessens and all becomes one, your new life now,
will have begun.
The role of the priestess is released upon you, daughter of Avalon
your energy anew.
The ancient soul awakened inside, I will walk with you now but as
your guide.
The words of the Mother resonate deeply within, as I embrace the
power that gently begins.

)O(

In the silent Hush

In the silent hush of the sacred space, she knows she is not alone
in this blessed place.
She can feel the ancients at her side, as she crafts their wisdom
that they guide.
Candle lit and incense burn, she chants her words as the energy
turns.
The heady scent fills the air, as she calls the spirits that dwell
within there.
The gentle Earth moves at her feet, as she walks in tune to the
pulsing heart beat.
Awakening the ancient soul within her bone, The priestess of
Avalon is never alone.
Crafting magic with the lore of the land, as the energy rises
through her outstretched hand.
The inner truths of the seer's eye, she looks within on a deepened
sigh.
She calls forth her sisters now, as they come together bound by
the sacred vow.
Energy rises to the point of creation, the power is released in pure
elation.
The priestess now in perfect bliss, seals the circle with an
enchanted kiss.
To Avalon now she does return, the way of the Goddess always to
learn.
)O(

Around me is a Gentle Cold

Around me is a gentle cold, I have heard about this in stories of old.

It wraps me in a nurturing embrace, and I open my eyes to see her face.

The peaceful mother is at my side, she knows of her I will abide.

She walks with me until I find my pace, that leads me away from the human race.

Through the mists to a land of long ago, here my soul belongs of this I know.

With my sisters and Mother in service to her name, I cleanse my being in the eternal flame.

Within this space now I will stay, throughout the night and of everyday.

I walk alone within the realm of man, but we are strong of the Avalon clan.

The mists are ours to lift as we choose, relieving the rays of the sacred hues.

The land so green and imbued with the fae, with the Moon of the night and the sun of the day.

This enchanted place within my heart, nothing will ever more keep me apart.

)O(

Within the heart of the humble seed

Within the heart of the humble seed is the beauty and wonder of
the majestic flower and all it will ever be.
Within the heart of your soul is the seed of your life, one to nurture
and grow as your path takes it's many turns.
But remember this seed was placed within your heart by the Great
Mother, she knows who you can be and has entrusted you with
this little seed.
For she knows you will grow it to its greatest beauty.
Trust that you are blooming for all to see, and you will grow into
the best you can be.

For she who knows all walks by your side, she protects and
illuminates your way.
Allow her to feed your soul and you walk your path and to fertilize
your dreams.

)O(

Forest Bright

Forest bright and emerald green, the place of where the ancestors dream.

The forest floor awake with night, the place of the fae and of the sprite.

Magic within and around this space, as the energies rise in a sacred place.

Where the witch has stood so often before, with her tools of the craft at her feet on the floor.

Within her hands the ancient power, that she calls upon in the moonlit hour.

Head of spells and body of light, she crafts and weaves her magic at night.

Cone of power rising high, she releases her craft within the skies.

The spell is worked and the magic is done, she returns now to where she begun.

Forest bright and emerald green, the place where the ancients have been.

)O(

I stand a while

I stand a while within my sacred space, with the silent hush of
nature caressing at my face.

The song of the Great mother whispers truths in my ear, the longer
that I stand here it all becomes so clear.

The messages from the familiars are showing me the way, how I
must walk alone as I tread my path today.

The ancient Priestess that lives within my heart, journey's by my
side as I breathe into my part.

The role of the cycle that I live by and obey, grows stronger and
more familiar as day passes day.

The elementals are rising as the power returns to the lands, we all
hold our power within our very hands.

Connecting now is such an important thing, the call of the
Priestess its her time to begin.

)O(

The Magpie Spoke To Me

The Magpie spoke to me and whispered the words of the ancients
within my ear.
I repeated them upon the words of my breath.
As they weaved their way into the world, I became priestess, I
became her, I became warrior.

As I walk my path today I walk with the ancestors by my side.
Within the beauty of the Great Mother I see her face within the
leaves and in the blossom upon the trees.

The green man places his hand gently upon my back, I feel
his strength throughout my body with every step I take.
Within my power I hold the elements and the secrets of the Sacred
path.

I am a Priestess and I will honour her within my life and path.
I only have to look within to see all I hold. For I need no man of
modern times to tell me my name.

I bow only to the name of the
old ones. The mother priestess and the Hunter by her side. I am
priestess. I am me. I am free.

)O(

She stands within the Ancient Woods

She stands within the ancient woods, the place where once her
ancestors stood.
The energies dancing around her hands, she holds the power of
the forgotten lands.
To pass her by is a mistake indeed, to bow and to honour you
must take heed.
For although she looks simple and fair, she is imbued with magic
if you stop and stare.
The mighty priestess from the sacred Isle, her magic released
with a nod and a smile.
She raises her hands and a fire is born, to work her rite on this
springtime morn.
In the sacred spring she holds the seers gaze, as the mists
descend in a enchanted haze.
Through the mists her sisters have come, to the call of the
energies they have succumbed.
The circle is drawn and the rite begins, with my heart and soul, I
step within.

)O(

Within my soul is the knowledge of old

Within my soul is the knowledge of old and ancient power of times
gone by.
The holder of wisdom and lore, the dragons whispered to me as I
silently slept within my mothers womb.
They told me of my lives gone by and who I truly was. They
showed me Avalon and the secrets she held and allowed me to
see the sacred truths.

I came to this place knowing who I was and tread my path with
power. By my side is the enchanting unicorn who guides my
course.
Who has stood with me when I was most alone, who protected me
when I felt fear and pain,
who gently nuzzled me when I needed reminding of how love
feels.

Now I honour the Goddess and Great Mother within everything I
do, for within her face I see myself, my life and path.
The fae dance freely around my feet, allowing magic and
enchantment to bloom with every step I take.

I no longer dwell within this realm.
Choosing to reside within Avalon as her priestess, her daughter
and pupil.
For she is me, and I am her.
Embrace the Great Mother within your soul as you walk your path
today.

)O(

She Stands Alone

(short version)

She stands alone, no one there but her.
She feels the pulse of the Earth beneath her feet.
The rains falls softly upon her face, reminding her of the emotions
that course throughout her body.

The wind gusting around her. The clouds break and the gentle
spring sun dances upon her face, reminding her of the heat and
passions to come as the land renews its cycle.
Bringing the wisdom of the ancients to her very being.
The dancing flame of the mighty fire warms her within, bringing a
passion to her magical workings.

As she gazes upon Avalon she draws this energy to every part of
her soul.
Feel the magic, for she sends it to you.

)O(

She stands alone, no one there but her

She stands alone, no one there but her.
She feels the pulse of the Earth beneath her feet.
The rains falls softly upon her face, reminding her of the emotions
that course throughout her body.

The wind gusting around her. The clouds break and the gentle
spring sun dances upon her face, reminding her of the heat and
passions to come as the land renews its cycle.
Bringing the wisdom of the ancients to her very being.
The dancing flame of the mighty fire, warms her within, bringing a
passion to her magical workings.

As she gazes upon Avalon she draws this energy to every part of
her soul.
Her heart beats as one with the gentle earth.
The ancients whisper softly within her ear, she knows what must
be done, for she is the priestess of the old.

The wise dragon stands sedately by her side consumed by the
magic within her being.
The unicorn stood on the other, pure of magic and true of heart,
both connected to her soul.
Her familiars trusting and faithfully by her side.
She is priestess. Feel her magic and embrace it for she sends it to
you.

)O(

Within my heart dwells a sacred truth

Within my heart dwells a sacred truth.
Within my soul lies an ancient path.
Within my hands I hold the ancestors power.

I am all that has gone before.
I am all that I can be.
I am all that is still to come.

I see the unseen.
I hear the unheard.
I speak the unspoken.

I walk beside the Great Mother and Father.
I carry the energy of the goddess within my body.
I am the hunter when I need my strength.

I am priestess of the old.
I am the witch of the ancient ways.
I am the healer of the herb lore.

I am mother.
I am healer.
I am teacher.

My soul lives within Avalon.

My energy bows to the wise ones.

My body listens to the great lady.

I am enriched beyond measure.

I am powerful beyond power.

I am gentle beyond grace.

I am priestess.

I am.

)O(

Within my heart (long version)

-

I am born of the Earth and the energy she gives me.
I am washed within water and the emotions I carry.
I am fuelled by fire and harness the energy of the passion.
The air flows through my being as the wisdom awakens my
soul.

Spirit walks with me, every step and turn.
Of the elements I am balanced and whole.
Alone I feel with my space the solitary one.
At times my sisters walk with me and Avalon.

Always of the Great Mother I am one.
Surrounded by the gifts of the land.
The familiar who walks by my side.
The answer to my question if I still to hear it.

Within my heart dwells a sacred truth.
Within my soul lies an ancient path.
Within my hands I hold the ancestors power.
I am all that has gone before.

I am all that I can be.
I am all that is still to come.
I see the unseen. I hear the unheard.
I speak the unspoken.

I walk beside the Great Mother and Father.
I carry the energy of the Goddess within my body.
I am the hunter when I need my strength.

I am priestess of the old.

I am the witch of the ancient ways.

I am the healer of the Herb Lore.

I am mother.

I am healer.

I am teacher.

My soul lives within Avalon.

My energy bows to the Wise ones.

My body listens to the great lady.

I am enriched beyond measure.

I am powerful beyond power.

I am gentle beyond grace.

I am she , who is of all things.

I am her who seeks the knowledge of the old ways.

I am Priestess. I am.

)O(

What is blessed be

What is Blessed be ?.
It is I honour the priestess within you.
I welcome the strength of the priest and the horned one.
I respect the path you have walked and how far you have
travelled.
I bow to the ancients by your side.
I see the lord and lady within your soul.
I hear your sacred breath of knowledge and of wisdom.
I feel the magic and enchantment around you.
I abide by the elementals and the power and lessons they bring.
I have connected to you from a sacred time.
We have walked together for many miles, sometimes alone and
sometimes connected but always as one.
I am bound to the secret of the dark nights and mystical moon.
Of the mists that part to reveal the secrets of herb lore and of
familiars wisdom.
I embrace the Elements and the wisdom they hold.
I walk and acknowledge the path of the ancients and wise.
I am part of the whole and all of everything.
I am the daughter of the Great Mother and of the Great Father.
Within my heart I carry the sacred truths.
I acknowledge this with two magical words,
Blessed be.

)O(

Blessed is my soul that has followed this path I walk upon

Blessed is my soul that has followed this path I walk upon.

Blessed are my feet that have carried me on my journey of the Lord and Lady.

Blessed are my legs that have kept me going when I wanted to turn back.

Blessed are my knees that kneel at the sacred altar.

Blessed is my womb that carries the seed of life within it.

Blessed is my heart that beats the ancient rhythm.

Blessed are my arms that embrace the energy around me.

Blessed are my hands that hold my power within them.

Blessed be my lips that speak the ancient truths.

Blessed are my eyes that give me the sight of the seer.

Blessed be my body and soul that honour the way of the priestess.

Blessed be my learning from the wise.

Blessed be my kin of the fae and of the unicorn without whom I would not be.

Blessed be my joy of walking daily with the Great mother and Father by my side.

Blessed be the wisdom I have learnt and yet to learn.

Blessed be the lessons that have given me the knowledge of who I am.

Blessed be the Great Mother for all she is and will ever be.

)O(

In My Heart I hold a simple truth

In my heart I hold a simple truth, one that is as ancient as time
itself.
The truth is that I follow my path without deviation or turn.
I am priestess of times forgot, of lands filled with the fae, of
enchantment and magic.
Where the unicorn walks and the dragon resides and power is the
sacred breath.
Times told in myth and in fables of old, is where my soul belongs.
I will not hide within the time for no man or belief.
I will walk my path as the priestess of the old ways, the ancient
craft and of the wise lore.
But I will watch as I see the young become lost and without
purpose.
And when the time is right and the seek the ways of the old, I will
be here to guide them.
The wise woman who is often misunderstood.
With the knowledge within her hands and the seer's gaze within
her eyes.
She who sees all but will not interfere unless she is called upon.
For our time is returning, the time of Avalon.
Of the priestess and Great Mother, we have only been but
sleeping.
Walking with our own kin of the sacred path.
I embrace my power, my energy within this time.
I am priestess.

)O(

The Sacred energies are coming back to the land

The Sacred energies are coming back to the land.

I feel the power growing within my hand.

The ancient mysteries are becoming clear.

The return of the Unicorns is coming near.

A time when all the realms become one.

The time of the old religion nearly begun.

The dragons and fae are returning now.

And to them I turn in honoured bow.

For Avalon now is shining through the mists.

The call of the Great Mother I cannot resist.

All becoming one and one becoming all.

I answer the song that my soul hears call.

)O(

Within my hands if I take a look

Within my hands if I take a look, is no ordinary looking book.
One that was passed from mother to kin, do I hold the strength to look within?
For on these pages is the knowledge of the wise, words from the land and of the sacred skies.
Ancient calls and words of power, I can conjure them all within this hour.
Magical rites and chants of old, stories of secrets never been told.
This book I will treasure for ever more, in honour of the priestess who have gone before.
My book of Shadows will always be, placed within my home most carefully.

)O(

Within the mists I am all I can be

Within the mists, I am all I can be.
The Great Mothers magic all around me.
My enchanted soul is blessed by the land.
As the wise woman takes my hand.
She leads to a quietened place.
As we honour the olds in this sacred space.
She empowers me with the ancient rights.
That can only be found upon the darkened night.
Lit only by the moon of above.
My heart is filled by the Goddess love.
For love of myself is the first right to learn.
To open the path that I have yearned.
For the priestess is an empowered soul.
With power and magic as her goal.
The ancient wisdom runs through my veins.
As I work my magic in the wise ones names.
The mists surround me and take me home.
But I know I will never be alone.

)O(

May your path be blessed

May your path be blessed as you walk its distance.

The Great Mother shadow's every step.

The Father of the hunt bring strength to your heart.

The Mother Priestess bring blessings to you in every way.

Blessed be dear one.

)O(

The Goddess welcomed me with a smile upon her face

The goddess welcomed me with a smile upon her face.
My heart was beating strongly as my soul filled with grace.
In her service I now belong I honour and obey.
I see her in the world around as I follow her gentle way.
The great mother lives in me and shows me how to be.
I bless the day she found my soul and awakened me to see.
I now walk my path illuminated by the light.
And celebrate my love for her even on the darkest night.
Alone or with my sisters I shall always be.
A Priestess to the goddess is the only path for me.

)O(

From the darkened days where the ancients walked

From the darkened days were the ancients walked,
The knowledge was passed from folk to folk.
Not a word was written down.
But whispered tales were told around town.
The woman of the wise and the man of song.
Kept our ancestry going strong.
But over time the stories of old .
Began to be feared as they were told.
The healing woman and her peaceful ways.
Saw the end of her solitary days.
Hunted and tracked by those she had helped.
Alone and abandoned is now all she felt.
Her days now ended in pain and in fear.
Of her I will not forget within my tear.
For she walked the path with honour and rite.
Gentle wise woman of the night.

)O(

The sacred symbols are drawn upon me.

The sacred symbols are drawn upon me, as I embrace this
powerful and wise energy.
Within my soul is the knowledge of old, that embraces me within
the Priestesses fold.
I will walk my path alone or with kin, but I walk the path holding the
truths within.
I hold my hand for those who seek, My promise to you I will always
keep.
To teach you all the ancient truths, that I have carried with me
since my youth.
The love of the Great mother is ours to share, If we open our
hearts if only we dare.
Avalon awaits for those who seek, the ancient secrets are ours to
keep.
Walk the path of the gentle priestess, to lead a life that is truly
blessed.
One of balance and the magical lore, to rekindle the time that has
gone before.
The time is right and the time is now, as I recognise you with the
humble bow.
Priestesses come walk with me, as we become all I know we can
be.

)O(

We have walked together you and I

We have walked together you and I, under many moons and starlit sky.

Through many places we have been, and all the stories we have seen.

Bound by the oath of the ancient lore, I hold your soul within my core.

My sweet dear sister of the craft of old, I have found you now and your energy I enfold.

In every lifetime I had before, I have looked for you within the ancient folklore.

We found each other every time, but it is sublime within this lifetime.

To bring forth the tales of old, of our rites, ways and belief to unfold.

Within your arms I feel safe once more, as we gaze beyond the mighty Tor.

To the realm of Avalon through her sensual mists, to where we cannot deny nor resist.

The call of our soul, the Mother and the priestess, were we feel the loving, giving caress.

The mighty power of the elders and wise, bound always by their ancestral ties.

Sister of mine I hold you so dear, as our path ahead becomes so clear.

)O(

When I draw that sacred breath

When I draw that sacred breath that others dare not to take.
I step aside from the realm of man, and the ancient path I tread.
The one that calls to me in the darkness of my dreams.
The mighty road of Avalon unfolds her path for me.

The more I age and become my years, here I can no longer stay.
For within the realm of man I have no place to be.
But within my home between the realms, the space of the
silver mists.
I am the wise old sage, embraced, welcomed and loved.

My sisters step with gentle walk as they dwell within the veil.
They bow their head in honoured turn as they respect the gift of
she.
The breath of life revives my soul and nourishes me so deep.
I no longer find what I need within the life of man.

The great Mother who is seen within all life and answers our call.
Never leaves our side but often allows us to fall and stumble.
We have to find our strength to regain our balance and stand.
The Mother Priestess always there but often out of sight .

To Avalon I long to be within my waking hours.
To descend the mists around my feet at a moment of my need.
To be within the time of the priestess and of magic and the fae.
To honour the divine feminine every hour as I wake.

I am alone right now, my sisters no longer here.

The web of light has dimmed once more and I feel them stand back once more.

My hand outstretched for the final touch before she hides her face.

I live with you within my heart and on every beat it makes.

)O(

The priestess walked along the path

The priestess walked along the path, she had trod so often before.
Listening to the song of the land and of the wise woman lore.
She picked her herbs as she made her way down the lonely
travelled path.
Longing for her covenstead and the warmth of the hearth.
Magic is a lonely life but blessed by all around, from the birds
within the sky and the animals of the ground.
To harness such a power of the elements in the hand, to feel the
gentle breath of the sacred land.
To walk the path of the ancients, and those who have gone
before.
The freedom of the priestess, hers for evermore.

)O(

Within the heart of the ancient soul

Within the heart of the ancient soul, dwells wisdom and magic of a
forgotten time.
We search for the Isle that burns in our lives, with the light of the
flame of Avalon.
Embers of the fire from within the veil, scattered across land and
time.
One day she will rise above the mists, bringing her children safely
home.

We are not the forgotten ones or the ones that time forgot.
We are the awakened souls of the priestess and priests of the
elders time.
We have within our souls and hearts the energy and knowledge of
old.
Now is the time to free ourselves and step from the realm of man.

Stand before her children of the old ways and honour her sacred
rites.
For now we see she of all things, within our eyes and mind.
Free her upon the breath of your words and within your daily
chore.
She of many names, but the Great Mother Goddess to all.

The sacred union between hunter and huntress dwells within our
loins.
We give birth to them within our lives and bring freedom to one
and all.
As the mystic Isle rises up to be in her rightful place, sister and

brother stand together .
Hand to hand and eye to eye in the circle of the old's.

We listen as we stand of the tales that went before.
To bring them to the modern lands, the mysteries of the wise.
We hear the call of the Avalon crone and we honour and obey.
The priestess of the sacred Isle, silently walks her path always.

The knowledge that she holds within, so pure of high intent.
The power of the essence she holds within her hand.
To empower the elements and the realm of the forgotten lands.
Her time is now, to rise up through the mist, to be seen for
evermore.

No longer hidden in time, beyond the reach of the ones that cannot
see.
Free to walk the worlds of mystical beast and magical kingdoms.
To hold the whispers of the ancient lore within her silent words.
To honour the ancients with every step and bring her teachings to
all.

)O(

I am borne of the earth

I am born of the earth and the energy she gives me.
I am washed within water and the emotions I carry.
I am fuelled by fire and harness the energy of the passion.

The air flows through my being as the wisdom awakens my soul.
Spirit walks with me, every step and turn.
Of the elements I am balanced and whole.

Alone I feel with my space the solitary one.
At times my sisters walk with me and Avalon
Always of the Great Mother I am one.

Surrounded by the gifts of the land.
The familiar who walks by my side.
The answer to my question if I be still to hear it.

Within my heart dwells a sacred truth.
Within my soul lies an ancient path.
Within my hands I hold the ancestors power.

I am all that has gone before.
I am all that I can be.
I am all that is still to come.

I see the unseen.
I hear the unheard.
I speak the unspoken.

I walk beside the Great Mother and Father.

I carry the energy of the Goddess within my body.

I am the hunter when I need my strength.

I am priestess of the old.

I am the witch of the ancient ways.

I am the healer of the Herb Lore.

I am mother.

I am healer.

I am Teacher.

My soul lives within Avalon.

My energy bows to the wise ones.

My body listens to the great lady.

I am enriched beyond measure.

I am powerful beyond power.

I am gentle beyond grace.

I am she, who is of all things.

I am her who seeks the knowledge of the old ways.

I am Priestess. I am.

)O(

I hold your hand within my own

I hold your hand within my own and together we become.
Away from this place and time we leave and to the mists we do
succumb.
Within the swirls I leave all I know behind in a gentle step.
I embrace the energy of Avalon with the ancient wisdom at its
depth.

I find myself upon the mossy banks of the deepest greatest lake.
I look within the mighty water as I see the journey to take.
I step into the waters deep and they wash away my fears.
As the nurturing Mother Goddess caresses and wipes my tears.

To be welcomed in the place I have searched for all my life.
A home I felt I would never find through all my pain and strife.
A different soul I have always been , on my own for many a year.
Yet embraced and welcomed, I have only felt deep love here.

This home I have found behind the mists one from ancient tales.
The wise and ancient souls from Avalon they do hail.
To be a part of this wondrous Isle is a gift I cannot deny.
Of the sacred oath and forgotten path I shall live my life by.

I am a priestess of the old ways and of the ancient lore.
I breathe the Goddess into my life as I embrace her and more.
With every step and every breath I enfold into the enrapture.
Of the beauty of my sacred home within my past,
present and future.

In my darkness and when I am alone, Avalon rise within this space and time.
To lift me when I need her most, ever within my heart and mind.
I know I am not alone, for my sisters I always find.
For we speak from the sacred tongue and of the heart and mind.

Gentle Mother who always walks by my side.
My loving teacher and ever my truthful guide.
Lead me to the place of old where I can be at one and free.
Where I am a priestess of Avalon and I can always be me.

)O(

She of the old ways

She of the old ways, of everything that was and everything to come.

She of the ancient path of magic and lore.

She of the silent folk of the fae and of the night.

She who holds the power of the elements within her hands.

The lady of the circle whose word is soft and true.

The lady of the cauldron whose power is intense.

The lady of the sight, whose eye never tells a deceit.

The lady of the many who is equal among the men.

The priestess of the craft from the time of long ago.

The priestess of the new souls who guides along the path.

The priestess of the familiar who listens to the call. The priestess of the Lord and lady who bows to their knowledge.

Who is she who walks this path? She lives within you and within me.

She is the divine ancient soul of the Great Mother that runs though our veins.

She is the breath of the morning breeze, the whisper within the bird song.

The glowing sun upon your face, The warming fire within your hearth.

The gentle shower of the spring rain and the torrential rains of the fall.

She is the balance within us and around us.

She is the truth within our hearts.

I will honour her with every breath and every step, for to be without her is not to live at all.

)O(

I stand within the elements

I stand within the elements, my feet upon the earth, the Great
Mother blesses me with her loving mirth.
The cleansing rains fall heavily upon my body and soul, through
this wild weather I take my freeing stroll.
The raven stands alone and watches as I pass, he stands within
the ancient stones embedded in the grass.
He nods his wisoned head and his eyes gives off a glint, of the
magic and wisdom he holds I see but just a hint.
I hear the words of the Lady, from Avalon she does hail, I see her
stood before me within her hands the grail.
Do I take the drink and become all I can be?. I call the elements
around me to help me clearly see.
The skies are laden with magic the hue is almost black, the rain
still lashing around me, on my face and back.
I feel her within each drop the life giving Mother Priestess, she
asks me the question and my answer can only be yes.
I follow her to Avalon my home for ever more, to be with my kin
and those who have been before.
Many blessings of the Goddess.

)O(

My cold breath upon the day

My cold breath upon the day, reminds me of who I am.
I find myself within this realm but filled with with the emotions and
memories of my beloved home , Avalon.
The coldness of winters grip, her icy hand embraces me and
guides me upon my path.
Within the realm of nature I am all I can be, as I gather the bounty
to adorn my home.
The mother has given such wondrous life and now as I pick up her
fruits, the very essence of the gift of life I hold within my hand.
The magical cells that are within my being have been within me for
as long as time.
To the lady my heart has always belonged and my soul has only
one heart that lies in Avalon.
Everyday that I walk this realm Avalon seems a step further away,
but I know that she is within the very essence of my breath.
I lift the mists to be home once more to walk the sacred ground.
Where I can be all I am without question, without fear and without
prejudice.
The gentle priestess who is the daughter of the old ways, but the
mighty warrior when roused.
I have much to teach, to give and learn and step aside from the
mists once more.
To become all I know I can be, and embrace my being to the core.
My cold breath upon the day, reminds me of who I am, I am she
who lives within me.

)O(

All that is between me

All that is between me and my beloved home stands the mighty
lake of Avalon.
As I stand before her she greets me within the mists and asks me
to lay bare my soul.
All I have gained and all I have become must be removed and
released.
She sees through to my core and all that lies within, all I cannot
see.

I stand before her dressed only within the robes of the priestess.
All I have and need is already within me.
The mists rise around my being consuming me, shrouding me from
the realm of man.
The energy quickens and I become.

Her of the Unicorns rises from the soft damp green mossy banks
of the lakes.
The mists are behind me and now I am home.
Avalon shimmers within the moonlight, she breathes life into my
heart.
I breathe her into me and all I was becomes whole.

I am Avalon, she is me. As I walk with each step I take, my feet
leave the ground.
I fly within the vortex of the power of this realm.
The winds bring the music from the lonely flute, on Celtic hearts
does it play.
Avalon in her full rite overlaps the realms for those that seek.

Drawing them in if they chose to follow the path.

For me that path always leads me home and I answer the question that I face.

I am daughter of the olds, woman of the wise, she of the ancients.

Before me are the Elders and after me are the learned.

I take my truth within my soul as I draw the sacred symbol upon my brow.

For to be embraced within Avalon is to be.

)O(

In the stillness of the night

In the stillness of the night I feel your touch within my heart.
Two souls entwined and ones that will never part.
The oath we took in the days of old before the Lady of the Lake.
Through the times of life and the journey's we would take.
Within the Raven and the crow upon their silent wing.
I hear the voice of Avalon as she begins to sing.

Daughter of the ancient ways and Priestess of the old.
Time to reveal the secrets that our Celtic soul does hold.
The Mist is lifting slowly and Avalon is near.
The twisting, winding and lonely path is becoming oh so clear.
We are being called to the Lady of the sacred isle once more and
work the realm of magic that we walked within before.

Sister of the blessed mist of the blue sickle moon.
The time to reveal ourselves is not a moment to soon.
Avalon she rises now to the height of her full.
Hear her call through the night and feel her mystic pull.
Through space and time ,world and land, over water and the sea.
We find each other as we awaken and allow us all to be.

Priestess of Avalon now it is our time.
Through the spoken word, chants and spellbinding rhyme.
Walk you path with knowing as we connect together once more.
Bringing the way of the Goddess to the gentle earth once more.
The Isle is awaiting for her children to return, bringing the bounty of
our journey's and all that we did learn.

)O(

I hail from the lands behind the mists

I hail from the lands behind the mists, that no sacred soul could
ever resist.
Of ancient hill and wayward rise, the magic is seen throughout the
skies.
The raven and crow on silent wing, tell tales of old that the elders
bring.
To walk the path behind the wise, I begin to see she in her Avalon
guise.

To Albion her heart belongs, yet throughout the world they hear
her song.
The secret whisper upon the winds, just heard once and your
journey begins.
To follow the lady to the sacred isle, is an arduous journey of many
a mile.
The knowledge and wisdom that her love brings, allows the heart
of the Priestess to sing.

When you lose your way and all seems lost, she awaits for you
behind winters frost.
She lifts the veil and releases the mists, within the energy here
your soul is kissed.
Of the Priestess lore and of the Priest's rites, magic is raised upon
the night.
She awaits for you now to welcome you home, for within her realm
you are never alone.

)O(

I remember such a long time ago

I remember such a long time ago, being visited by the one I know.
A wise old sage with a kindly face, born of the ancients and of the
Avalon race.
He told me tales of long ago, ones I had forgotten, but of them I
know.
He told me I was a child of the ancient path, with magic and
wisdom within my heart.

Those childhood days seem so distant vague, yet I remember him
well the wise old sage.
He often came when I was alone, when within this realm I wasn't at
home.
I dreamt of an Isle on a distant shore, one I had walked so often
before.
Of the mother and Lady and of enchanted realm, from the mighty
oak to the gentle elm.

The ancient guide who seeks his kin, ones of wisdom and who
welcome him in.
To the mighty realms he returns their soul ,walking his path and
fulfilling his role.
He has walked with me from that day to this, through the
darkened days to the ones of bliss.
By my side he is forever more, the Merlin ,my father, he of
folklore.

)O(

She stands aloft the windswept cliff

She stands aloft the windswept cliff, the elements dancing around
her feet.
She summons the energy within her soul, and chants a rhythmical
beat.
Her robes billow within the winds and the energies begins to rise.
She lifts the mists before her face and Avalon is within her eyes.

The call of magic is upon the wind as the sacred rite weaves
across the skies.
She protects herself and her working space she walks her circle
clockwise.
The ancient ones hear her call and around her they surround.
By her oath to the Goddess her workings are always bound.

She calls upon the elders and those who have walked before.
As she cast her magical workings under the ancient lore.
Gentle priestess alone and within her mighty power.
Working from her knowledge within this enchanted hour.

She casts her workings into the night and sets them free to soar.
And releases them to the energies born of old folklore.
Avalon born and mystical bred, she holds the knowledge of old.
Beware of the gentle priestess and of all the secrets she holds.

)O(

From the path of the old

From the path of the old, and craft of the wise,
I have travelled this land under many skies.
From my small little cottage at the edge of the wood,
The wise women alone and misunderstood.
I crave for my solitude and just to be, as I carve my spells full of
mystery.
With my herbs all gathered and hanging to dry,
I offer my healing to those that pass by.
As I call upon dragons and ancient gods,
Following the path the unicorns trod.

)O(

I am Avalon Born

I am Avalon Born, of the Sacred Isle and of the enchanted mists,
I have followed my path of many turns and often heartbreaking
twists.
They have lead me to the place of where I am today,
Not a thing I would do again not in any way.

To find acceptance within the realm of where I dwell and walk,
Looking for the words of love as I listen to the folk that talk.
Releasing the call of judgment that I place upon myself,
The energy I have held onto and placed within body and my
health.

No longer do I shy away from my path and of my light.
I hold the colour of Avalon a blue shining light.
The time of the child who is lost to all around,
I embrace her fully now as her soul I have found.

I see you with me and together we do walk,
As we connect once more and hold the balanced talk.
I hear your words and they open the doors I locked so tight,
I release the shadow that held the fear of the night.

The Lady she has beckoned me to teach her sacred word,
To bring it to those who as yet have unheard.
I am the Priestess of Avalon in so many ways,
I chose to follow her path till the end of my days.

)O(

Within the Shadow of the pool

Within the shadow of the pool I find myself alone, with a growing
distant memory of my beloved home.
The shadows of the sisters are held within the mists, the reaching
of their hand to mine I no longer can resist.
The sadness within my heart of the ancient ways and time, no
matter how hard I look today I no longer find.

The energy of Avalon the sacred Isle and haven, I find the
message of she upon the wing of the raven.
The ancient memory of a peaceful place to reside, I know I will find
again if I reach deep inside.
The priestess within my soul can no longer hide away, to be within
Avalon once more I must walk my path today.

To connect with my sisters who hold the sacred rites, under the
moon laden sky on the darkest starlit night.
The energy of Avalon she pulls me more each day, as she reaches
out to this lost child and shows her the way.
The path before me opens and the mists lift for me to see, my
home stands before me and within Avalon I be.

)O(

Through the times when I lose the most

Through the times when I lose the most, I find myself alone,
The journey consumes me and binds my hope and to that I must
atone.
Within myself I journey, to find the mystic path.
To find the one who knows me, with the honest and open heart.

Through the changing seasons and within the day and night,
The Earth she has called me in the darkest of midnight.
Upon the many winds, and of the seasons four.
I have walked the road to the place I trust, and where my soul
adore's.

The Lady she did find me when my cry was but a word,
She lifted my head in her hands and told me that she had heard.
I wept upon her embrace as I realised I was home,
To be within Avalon, never again to walk alone.

The power and the passion of this enchanted space,
Is the essence of my life and of my rightful birthplace.
The oath I took and honour in the ancient days,
To work the line of magic and the ancient ways.

Forever more the priestess of the sacred mists,
With the love of my sisters I cannot resist.
To follow in the footsteps of those who have gone before,
To embrace the mystery of Avalon and teach her sacred lore.

)O(

Avalon awakes within her dawn

Avalon awakes within her dawn, she beckons the lost, lonely and forlorn.
She calls to you on the harshest breeze, her summoning power bringing you to your knees.
She awaits upon the pouring rain, when you have nothing left to gain.
When this realm no longer holds true, when you awaken to the gifts you hold within you.
The gates of the realm open with ease, and the ancient ones you now must appease.

It the dark of the night when all is asleep, your soul to her is allowed to keep.
To honour the oath of the sacred ways, the one you took in the priestess days.
Time to step from all you know, you release the past and wounded ego.
For here in this space and within this time, you must honour the vow that your soul does bind.
Only those who can find the mist, can step though and beyond to exist.

The knowledge and wisdom is yours to behold, and of the myth and story that was foretold.
For Avalon she is rising up again, within the woman, the child and the heart of the man.
Her ways and knowledge are being reborn, like the mighty oak within the acorn.

She will rise to her rightful place, of the old ways and lore full of wisdom and grace.

If she calls to you hear her cry, for to refuse her now you soul would deny.

The world is ready for the Priestess lore and of all the magic that has gone before.

Never before have we held our time, within our words and chanted rhyme.

To walk the earth in our rightful place, with the symbols drawn upon our face.

Empower your soul and your sisters you find, through the land, space and time.

Avalon rises more each day, her call is clearer in every way.

)O(

All around is a silent hush

All around is a silent hush, apart from the song of a small lonely thrush.

She sings to me and lifts my soul, the little bird by the feeding bowl.

She tells me all of the winters delights and urges me to seek the stars tonight.

For within the sky if I choose to see, are the spirits of the ancients looking down at me.

The long winters night I wear like a cloak, as I listen to the words that once I spoke.

Filled with wisdom, Insights and song, from a time and land from where I belong.

So as midwinter falls gently upon me, I embrace my soul and my life's journey.

)O(

As the Mists part today

As the mists part today, I find myself gazing upon my home. I feel a joy that warms the very essence of my soul. For my eyes fall upon Avalon. The feeling of warmth that I feel as I smell the world around me. No longer am I part of the reality I have stepped from. But part of a realm filled with magic, mystery, learning, and wisdom. Nature raises her head to great me and welcome me home. I look before me and see that all around me is enchanted with the fae. Today I will stay within this realm to rest and be healed. May you be blessed all day through in all that you do.

)O(

She stands within the ancient woods

She stands within the ancient woods, the place where once her
ancestors stood.
The energies dancing around her hands. She holds the power of
the forgotten lands.
To pass her by is a mistake indeed, to bow and to honour you
must take heed.
For although she looks simple and fair, she is imbued with magic if
you stop and stare.
The mighty priestess from the sacred Isle. Her magic released with
a nod and a smile.
She raises her hands and a fire is born. To work her rite on this
springtime morn.
In the sacred spring she holds the seers gaze, as the mists
descend in a enchanted haze.
Through the mists her sisters have come. To the call of the
energies they have succumbed.
The circle is drawn and the rite begins, with my heart and soul, I
step within.

)O(

When I feel lost

When I feel lost or even forlorn, I turn my face to the wakening dawn.
The lady she waits within the rising sun, and she holds my energy when I have none.
When I feel I have nowhere to turn, she hears my cry and my heart wrenching yearn.
She holds me in an embrace that only a mother can hold, as I weep and collapse into her loving enfold.

She calms my breath as my voice has no sound, and she catches my soul as I fall to the ground.
She whispers gently within my ear, "that all will be well my daughter so dear".
She gives me the strength of the life giving Earth, and I all am becomes a rebirth.
I feel her breath within my own, and within that moment I am no longer alone.

The Lady is with me within every step I take, of the choices and decisions that I choose and make.
She catches me every time I fall, and in the times to her I forget to call.
She waits for me in the moment to become, of the changing seasons from spring to Autumn.
I see her within everything I pass by, within the gentle flower and the stars in the sky.

The Mists always find me when I forget my way home, and take
me back to my beloved Avalon.
There she stands with her arms open wide, as into the circle I step
inside.
With a sigh that comes from the depths of my soul, and my spirit
and body becoming whole.
I stand as the priestess within my power, within every moment and
passing hour.

)O(

In The Emerald Isle

In the Emerald Isle, in the days of old, the priest died away.
His memories of an ancient path, became hidden and lost.
The priestess hidden in a fallen tear, no longer danced the Irish song.

Remember our kin on St Patrick's day, the day the heart of Albion died.
May all the children of Albion rise once more dear brother and sister.
Stand shoulder to shoulder as the way of the ancients shows us the path of the future.

As those who revel without a belief, we do rise from the ashes once more.
The Emerald Isle of the fae and dragon breathes within its core.
As the snakes return within their birth and awaken the sacred oath.

I am a Priestess of the old ways with my soul within the Irish bone.
I hold the shamrock aloft in the name of the maiden, mother and crone.
One day I will return to my Celtic home, with my kin by my side.
We will reclaim the ancient ways, the land, the sea and skies.
No longer within the dark of night or hidden within our fright.
We shall stand tall and proud on St Patrick's night.
Many blessings from the ancient and olds.

)O(

Whispers of the Festivals

Samhain

The wheel has turned, the wheel of light

The wheel has turned, the wheel of light, stoke the fire and make it
bright.
Samhain call, samhain come, feel the rhythm, hear the drum.
The veil it thins, the veil it shrouds, the spirits rise upon darkened
cloud.
The time of orange, time of black, time to move forward and not
look back.
Pumpkin lit, with candle burn, away dark spirits this guardian
turns.
Night of the ancients, night of the olds, remembered in stories now
to be told.
The crone doth rise upon this night, look into the shadows without
a fright.
Rituals and rites across the lands, empowers the soul where they
stand.
Trick or treat, heal or curse, the hand should be crossed from a
silver purse.
The wheel begins its time anew, the release of the old for the
knowledgeable few.
The time to scry to see the path we must take, and of the choices
we need to make.
She comes to us in many guises, the crow and the owl her
favorite disguises.
The Earth gives us her last to give, the bountiful harvest so we can
live.
We feast and drink in a sacred space, behind samhain masks to
hide our face.

Through darkened day and moonlight night all hallows eve is a beautiful sight.

)O(

Samhain marks my time upon this Earth

Samhain marks my time upon this earth, it will be many years
since my time of birth.
Through the swirling mists I chose to walk, and of the great mother
priestess I always talk.
I walk between realms and through the mists, how could I deny or
even resist.
The gift the lady bestowed upon me, to hear her whispers and set
them free.
To find myself within this place, has been a harrowing journey
through time and space.
One I would not change in a single way, for they created the soul I
am today.
Alone I have walked for many a mile, some folk I have passed
without even a smile.
Avalon born of the ancient race, within the world I see the Lady's
face.
Today I have grown into all I can be, a loving soul who's spirit is
Free.
Within my life the most wonderful friends, in each other's lives did
our energies wend.
The energies rise through the thinning veil, of loved ones we seek
as Avalon hails.
Have a blessed samhain one and all, hark to the crone as she
begins to call.

)O(

As we draw near to the end of the Celtic year

As we draw near to the end of the Celtic year, culminating in the
thinning of the veil at Samhain (all hallows eve).
Take this time to start reflecting on your past, present and future.
Look for guidance from the olds and your kin that has passed.
To how your journey will unravel in the new year.
Where do you want to go? What do you want to be?
Allow yourself to embrace your journey .

)O(

As the crone begins to awaken from her slumber

As the crone begins to awaken from her slumber,
The seasons roll from October to November.
The darkness falls all around,
The animal now are earthward bound.
The Holly and the Ivy the traditional flora,
Greens and reds the Earth's natural aura.
Candle light and roaring fires,
Warm even you smallest desires.
Family time by blood or by soul,
Come together allow the laughter to roll.
In the earths darkest days,
When we no longer see the suns warming rays.
Just come inside, gather one and all,
And celebrate the last days of Fall.

)O(

As the festival of Samhain continues today

As the festival of Samhain continues today.
We celebrate all souls day.
Time to pay homage to those that have passed.
Sending them back to the spirit realms with the warmth from our
hearts.
Having shown them our families, our growth and our lives.
Said the last word we didn't get the chance to speak.
And although they do not walk by our side in flesh and bone.
Just knowing that they walk with us daily within sprit and will return
to us next year at Samhain.

)O(

Pumpkins carved and candles lit

Pumpkins carved and candles lit,
The wood is laid in the sacred fire pit.
The spirits are rising, its the night of the dead,
By the light of the candle they will be led.
Raise a glass to the olds and for what they bring,
For Samhain is coming a time to sing.
Enjoy getting ready for this harvest festival,
For it signifies the end of Fall.

)O(

Yule....Winter Solstice

Holly Green and Berries red

Holly Green and berries red, resting gently upon my head.
Mistletoe hung way up high, We danced the dance the king and I.
Herne himself blessed our song, as we return to where we do
belong.
Yule fires burning across the land, as I am led gently by the hand.
Forest green and gentle face, I trust this guide with respect and
grace.
The Holly King my guide for now, to him I bend in honoured bow.
But soon at Yule I must let him go, and embrace the other that I
know.
The King of Oak will be with me, and the summer dance will begin
with glee.

)O(

The Holly and the Oak King

The Holly and the Oak King their battle just begun,
One will die away, the other the returning sun.
The fight within the cycle the two of them must duel,
With the Oak King winning, celebrating at Yule.
Soon will be midwinter, the harshest of all the times,
But surrounded by family and others of our kind.
Holly must be brought in to protect us and our kin,
The Yule log burning brightly, warning us within.
The Yule tree decorated brightly, reminds us of the light,
A merry festive season awaits before our sight.

)O(

Yuletide deepens at this time of year

Yuletide deepens at this time of year,
Filled with hope and happiness and cheer.
The time of the family, the old and the young,
The returning light, of the warmth and the sun.
Time to take stock of all you hold,
Time to ready with frankincense and gold.
To protect your home, your family and soul,
To renew your dreams, your wishes and goal.
The shortest day and longest night,
Is behind us now as we welcome the light.
The promise of what is yet to come,
Is wrapped in the gifts we give as our custom.
Festive laughter, fun and glee,
As we gather around the decorated Yule tree.
From the days of old, to the modern time,
We honour Yule with a sacred chime.
The priestess from within the mists,
Reflects the season with all its twists.
Time to rejoice in all that is done,
Yet to embrace the new and what is to become.
So dear sisters, brothers and kin,
Make ready your rite for your joy to begin.
Surrounded by those that you love,
As we honour the season below and above.

)O(

The snow is falling softly upon the ground

The snow is falling softly upon the ground, magic and enchantment
is all around.
A time for wonder, laughter and fun, the yuletide season just
begun.
The mistletoe and holly, the outside brought in, to protect your
home, friends and kin.
The solstice, time of the shortest day, a chance to be visited by
magic and fae.
Midwinter the time of the returning sun, fill your life with laughter
and fun.
The darkened days are all but done, let's celebrate the life of the
returning sun.

)O(

Twinkling lights upon the tree

Twinkling lights upon the tree, children's faces lit up with glee.
From ancient times this festival began, gathering of tribes, villages
and clan.
A time of family, feasting and fun, when the Holly King died and
the Oak King won.
Today it seems sometimes forgotten, the lore of the land the stores
lay rotten.
Lets remind them then just you and me, the true meaning of Yule.

)O(

As winters hands tighten her grip

As winters hands tighten her grip, from the cup of ice we take a sip.

A timely reminder for us all to bare, she hides her face behind long ashen hair.

She holds on tight the crone goddess, for winters cold heart, we must honour and bless.

Her wizened hand knarled but strong, holds us to the winter song.

Take stock of what you hold dear she cries, for what is mine I cannot deny.

I will withdraw it deep within the earth, till at spring new growth begins with mirth.

For now we must draw in tight and bless our souls till the returning light .

)O(

Cold and wet winters morn

Cold and wet winters morn, the wind lashing at the window pane.

Fierce and unforgiving at this time of year, the cold relentless rain.

As I look outside at the cold new day, the wilds of winter before
me.

I warm myself within my home, at one here I now be.

I yearn for the long days of the sun, but not to wish away the days.

For everything within in its time and place, even the warming rays.

For now I will watch the scudding skies and the tress as they
dance in the gales.

I will venture out later today, my cloak billowing like sails.

)O(

He waits for us to rest our tired and weary heads

He waits for us to rest our tired and weary heads, snuggled in
tightly within our cosy beds.

He then comes to play within the cold dark night, and weaves his
winters magic away from our sight.

They call him by his name through the darken hours, and casts a
magic spell through the winter flowers.

Sparkle white and sparkle bright on all that is laid bare, Jack frost
rides the clouds wizzing through the air.

Only in the morning when our eyes areopen wide, do we see the
beauty that waits for us outside?

)O(

I love this time of year

I love this time of year.
Excited children and smiling faces.
Thinking of others and buying things that will touch their hearts.
Bringing the green of the earth inside the home to decorate it for
the Yule festivities.
What a wonderful feeling.
Cupboards stocked.
The Yule tree decorated and lit to symbolise the returning sun.
What a warming feeling it gives me inside.
Enjoy your preparations for Yule time my friend.
Blessings for the winter solstice.
May the light return in your life threefold.
Bringing strength and growth in every aspect of your being.
As the light in your heart is rekindled by your family and loved
ones.

)O(

Imbolc

Out of the Darkness

Out of the darkness came the hands of light, the maiden stood
before my sight.
She lifted me up from the depths of the year, and on her breath
she told me Spring is near.
Time to move onwards and embrace all that is to come, take heed
of the newness that has begun.

The Earth she recovers from the harsh Winters days, as she
warms herself in the weak sun's rays.
So much hope and promise to be born, It is with lightness of foot
that my path I adorn.
She holds out her hand and reaches to mine, as our souls and
energy becomes entwined.

The newness the vitality reaches within ,as I await for this next
step of the journey to begin.
Out of the stillness of the dark winter days, I can feel the warm
summer in its haze.
She beckons me forward to awake in my soul, the time to think of
my distant goals.

The lady she whispers so loud and clear, "It is time for new growth
however it appears".
"The seeds you have planted have been waiting to grow, you
always reap what you do sow."
Allow the Mother to nurture you deep, release the old and what
you no longer keep.

Time of new beginnings for those who see, the time of the hermit
no longer for me.
The wheel of life has turned from dark to light, as the growing
energy leaves behind the night.
The energy quickens as new life is near, we hold in our hearts the
promise so dear.

Have a blessed Oimelc with you loved ones close, and of the Lady
and what she bestows.
Light a candle of the colour white, to chase away darkness and
night.
The wheel is turning already again, as we leave behind Winter and
her harrowing reign.

)O(

In the midst of winter there is a returning light

In the midst of winter there is a returning light.
One that brings hope and joy even on the darkest night.
As the wheel of life doth turn each day.
The signs of rebirth are on their way.
Place this new life within your heart.
Feel the new energy beginning to spark.
May the joys of spring flower around your soul.
As you begin to carve your path and goal.
Take notice of nature as she begins to bloom.
Sweep out your space with a cleansing broom.

)O(

Blessing to you on this beautiful day of Imbolc

Blessing to you on this beautiful day of Imbolc.
The day and time of new beginnings and balance.
A time when the great mother releases the new life she has been
nurturing within her belly.
A time of sweeping out the old negativities and releasing them to
the winds.
Watching the cleansing rains wash the last stubborn bits of the old
away.
A time of great protection given by Brighid to your home and your
family for the coming year.
Enjoy this gentle turn of the wheel that brings us much
Strength.
For now the light has truly returned.

)O(

I bring blessings today from the great mother

I bring blessings today from the great mother.
She asks that you sweep your life of negativities for the coming
months ahead.
It is time to let go of those things in life that hold you back,
physically, mentally and emotionally.
Plant a bulb that is just for you.
So as it begins to grow you can see the new beginnings coming
into your life.
Call upon the energy of the great mother to be with you.
Enjoy the freedom and growth that she brings into your life when
you allow her to.
Enjoy the world around you.

)O(

There is a quickening across the land

There is a quickening across the land.
The Goddess is making ready for new beginnings.
Are you ready? Have you swept away the old?
Released what you no longer need.
Take your lead from the Earth.
What hasn't survived the winter has withered and died.
Becoming compost for that what has survived deep within the
great mothers belly.
Feeding the new, young and tender life.
This is the time of the returning light.
Embrace it into your life and watch the new grow within and
around you.

)O(

Oimelc.... Spring Equinox

I can feel the Goddess awakening with every step I take

I can feel the Goddess awakening with every step I take.
Can feel her gentle kisses in the wind upon my face.
The gentle warming sun energises my soul.
Reminds me of the path I'm on to reach my given goal.
The animals are waking from the darkened days of winter.
The hold of the cold and dark now starts to splinter.
The quickening that is around us renews our strength and might.
Embrace at the equinox the return of the light.

)O(

The lady walks with me today

The lady walks with me today, she asks me to look deep within.
To release all that I no longer need.
For as I release all that holds me back, I become free.
The elements begin to balance and I become one with the great
Mother.
The power dwells within my soul.
I am Priestess.
I am the energy of Spring.

)O(

Beltane

Beautiful Blessings upon this May eve

Beautiful blessings upon this may eve. The time of the thinning
veil.
Connections to the other realms clearer and stronger.
As the energy courses through the great mother she becomes the
huntress, aligned only with the energy of the hunter.
Their sensual energy culminating in ecstasy at Beltane.
Their love as old as time and bringing passion and commitment
into our lives if we choose it.
All around can feel this energy rising.
Embrace it. As you light the great fires remember all that has gone
before and that which is still to come.
Remember to dance and bathe in the Beltane dew, to bring the
beauty of the goddess to you.
Blessings at Beltane.

)O(

As the mists rise and reveal all that lies beyond

As the mists rise and reveal all that lies beyond, I find myself within
Avalon once more.
My beloved home, where my soul resides, my lifetimes culminating
in this time of the Priestess right now.
Before me is the great wooden pyre of the Beltane fire, and aloft is
the wicker form, that represents all our manifestations and dreams.
And the return of the life giving sun. Within it are the heady scents
of incense and the floral offerings.
The drum starts its pulsating beat and we are heralded to
procession by the rhythmical chant of the Elders.

The Great Mother and Great Hunter lead the way to our sacred
ground, where the ancients have walked before.
As our hands rise aloft, the call of the elements is given, within our
hands we hold the orb of fire, that will light the Beltane right.
With one motion the orbs are given to the hungry wood, who
consumes them like a wild animal.

The chants give way to an empowered silence, as all give honour
to those that have gone before, the death and rebirth of our
ancestors.
The Hunter and Lady become one in their ritual of sensual love, as
they walk the circle of their children, we bow to their love and
bond.
The great rite carries on long into the night, and we work with the
thinning veil to scry into the past, the present and future.

Embracing the insights and treasuring the truths, we will work towards within this turn of the wheel.

With The Beltane fire alight within my heart and soul, I sit to rest under the mighty Yew tree.

My eyes begin to close and when they open once more I find the mists have descended.

I am within my home once more. With Avalon but just a breath away.

)O(

I feel the Energies rise

I feel the energies rise as the Beltane quickening flows through the skies.

Animals full of the summer to come. The god and the Goddess love full of frolic and fun.

A time to celebrate the fire deep inside, that has waited all winter after the sun God died.

The sensual pulse is rising through me, as I dance the maypole in abundant glee.

My whole body is awake for the first time this year, and the Celtic wheel turns my path it steers.

The ancient call is rising within me, to run through the woods with Hunter and the Fae.

I see them all around, from the sylphs of the Air, to the Gnomes of the ground.

The old magic is returning now, embrace it well as you take your bow.

The elements in their height of power, as we approach the time of Beltane hour.

)O(

Gentle Mother

Gentle Mother walk by my side as we celebrate the Solstice with ancient pride.

Dressed within your cloak of Green, the energies rise the Lord is seen.

The Father God full of energy and strength, upon this day of the longest length.

Litha fire burn within me as the warming sun awakens my energy.

We walk the path that the ancestors took, to the sacred space we take a look.

Solstice rise and solstice risen. The goddess child now is given.

The emerald lands full of colour, as we take our turn and give our honour.

The crops have grown and the harvest is full, as Lughnasaghd energy lends its pull.

The wise folk of the land raise their hearts within their hands.

Thanks and blessings are upon us now, as we turn the wheel our heads do bow.

Solstice blessings to one and all, but only if you hear the ancient call.

)O(

Lughnasagdh

The Wheel has slowly turned

The wheel has slowly turned as we readily reap all we have
learned.
The humble seeds we planted within, we nurtured with love for
growth to begin.
The first harvest of the year, allows us to see with eyes so clear.
All we have gained all we have grown, how the turning year seems
to have flown.
The seasons grew as we cherished our crops, and at times we
even seemed to stop.
But at lughnasadh time as the sun shines down, the god in his
height with his sun lit crown.
Illuminates our growth over the past seasonal year, that we
celebrate now with reverence and cheer.
Soon we will turn to the fall, and hear the crones whispered call.
Of darkened days and storm filled nights, and mid winter within it's
height.
So cherish now the last of the sun, and the harvest festivals that
have begun.

)O(

Blessings to you at this time of the first harvest

Blessings to you at this time of the first harvest.

I give you blessings that you find your harvest of you desires has grown into your reality.

Take the opportunity now of Sacrificing bad habits and unwanted things from your life .

By throwing symbols of them into the sabbat fire.

Have a magical Lughnasagh.

)O(

Mabon.... Autumn Equinox

The bony fingers of the Mother

The bony fingers of the Mother beckon the autumn to her breast, a
time of withdrawn reflection, of insight and much needed rest.
The sun becomes like water, reflecting and shimmering low, within
the cocoon of the Mother it soon will be our turn to go.
The cascading colours of Autumn, the aura of the Earth, making
ready for Winter and soon the lands rebirth.
The gather of the Harvest is nearly at its end, the festival of the
Equinox will be celebrated with friends.
Sister of Avalon make ready for the darkened days, the time of the
Mother Crone, and the teachings of the old ways.
The air is becoming crisp the light becoming short, yet my heart
skips a beat just at the very thought.
The days of the shadow will bring knowledge to all, and bound
within the energy of the season of the Fall.

)O(

The Autumn winds bring time of change for all

The Autumn winds bring time of change for all, the Mother
Goddess beckons to those who hear her call.
The trees begin to let go of all they no longer need, I take lessons
of the nature and of their teachings I take heed.
The God of light and of the warmth of the Sun, returns to the
mother's womb his resting time now begun.
The God of Dark and all we hold within, his time now comes for
his Winters reign to begin.
The Crone is before me and for the darkened days of the year,
time of reflections and scrying to see it clear.
As I gather in the harvest and make ready for what's to come, I
look outside the window and the fall has already begun.
The moon is waxing gently, soon she will rise to full, upon the night
of the equinox we will feel her magical pull.
The ancients that have walked before us opened the path up wide,
allow the withdrawing energy of the season to balance all within.
The Mists fall thickly around us and the Winter breathes her song,
the call of nature within us and to all they do belong.
Avalon retreats into the sighing skies, the Priestess wisdom is
seen within her eyes.
May you celebrate with love and surrounded by your friends, the
bounty of your harvest and of the summer's end.
The home is to be protected through the passing days, in the steps
of the ancients and of their sacred ways.

)O(

As the air becomes filled

As the air becomes filled with the mabon energies.
And the equinox brings balance into our lives.
The fall gives is a chance to let go of all that we hold close and no
longer serves us.
Find a place today and let go.
Bringing the balance to your soul. and reaping the bountiful
harvest you richly deserve.
The equinox is nigh.
And as I gather my harvest, leaves, acorns and conkers for my
thanks giving.
I feel warm inside.
The world is warm and glowing with abundance.
My face reflects the joy it see's and smiles at strangers .
The great mother is giving so much at this time.
That it makes me look at what I am giving, Is it too much? Is it
too little? can I give more?
I want to find the balance that surrounds me and bring it into my
life.
So at the equinox I will bring balance into my life.
Will you allow the energies of the equinox to evoke your soul.
As the God and Goddess, the Sun and Moon find balance within
themselves.
Find it within you and your life.
Balance the spiritual and physical.
Take just a moment and allow the energies to arise through your
body
Awakening all within.

)O(

As the leaves begin their gentle journey

As the leaves begin their gentle journey from the tree to the earth.

The autumn hush is all around.

The songbird sings his winter song.

And the animals now are earthward bound.

The autumn aura is a joy to see.

Feeding our souls, allowing us to be.

The turn of the wheel is upon us once more.

Winters heavy breath at the creaking door.

So prepare for the darkened days ahead.

Allowing the body to be led.

By the mystical dance of the seasons tune.

Energised by the sun and moon.

For the sun will return once more in spring.

With the whispers of a promise of new life a coming.

)O(

The Autumn rain has come today

The Autumn rain has come today.

To wash away the summer.

The last memories of the hazy days have become but a glimmer.

The spiders webs are tightly spun.

The winters spell now truly begun.

Have you taken the time to see what you no longer need.

Loose the baggage that will weigh you down throughout the darkened days.

Stock the cupboards, put the garden to bed.

Feed the birds and rest your weary head.

Everything slows at this time, even you and me.

So stop pushing yourself night and day and learn just to be.

)O(

Leaves and laughter

Leaves and laughter Autumn fun.
Playing away under the gentle sun.
The subtle frost shimmers at night.
An enchanted land a wondrous sight.
The fae are enchanting the land to sleep.
A winters slumber theirs to keep.
Take this time to look around.
A winters beauty yours to be found.
Slow a little and listen more.
As winter creeps to your door.
Shorter days and longer nights.
The solstice time is winters height.
So gather and store for your needs.
A time for your soul to nourish and feed.
To blossom anew at the time of light.
With longer days and shorter nights.
The wheel will turn forever more.
You're a part of the cycle within your core.

)O(

Whispers of the Enchanted Beasts

The Sleeping Dragon

The sleeping dragon raises his head, as the Priestess walks softly
by.
She caresses his head within her hands and she feels him give a
sigh.
This mighty beast as old as time, the keeper of the mystic realms.
Is lost to man upon this day as he no longer holds the helm.
His majesty and his power has earned him respect and grace.
But only within Avalon dare he show his face.
To walk among his kind and to be with his brethren and his kin.
The place of magic and enchantment is where his life begins.
Wise one so full of tales of the ancients and the olds.
Show us the path to follow as we watch the mists unfold.
To reveal this sacred and abundant land, that travels through time.
Only open and visible to those that read the signs.
The Priestess sits a while his nose nuzzled within her lap.
Her gentle stroking of his head allows him to rest and nap.
His mind wanders back in time to the days of when he reigned.
Through the doors and different lands he walked and always
gained.
Until the time that man forgot and found fear for his wizened friend.
The time of the dragon soon came to its end.
He now rests within the sacred isle within the land of the fae.
Waiting the time of calling to return when the dragon has his day.
Avalon and the Priestess protect him until this time.
Shrouding him within magic and the bonds that bind.

)O(

As he Stands ready

As he stands ready to call the Elders to arms.

He knows that this is his chance to walk the realms of the ancients.

Becoming seen once more.

For an eternity he has been banished from these realms.

As keeper of the sacred truths his wisdom was too much to bare.

He was forced to leave his beloved Celtic lands to reside between the mists.

Banished to the realm of the unseen, he fought bravely to return.

Only being seen within the eye of the magical.

His wisdom and power harnessed by those who are of the craft.

By only those who can hold his mighty power.

By those who are of his brethren.

Avalon stand tall amongst the dragon walkers.

Those of the ancestors tongue.

Those who honour and respect the wise one.

As the mighty Dragon looks within my eye.

He sees me.

He knows me.

For we have walked this path together many times.

We will walk together again.

As he rises to be seen once more.

)O(

As the mighty beast looked deep into my eyes

As the mighty beast looked deep into my eyes, he looked past my
humanity and deep within my soul.
I knew I could not hide myself from him. He who was as old as
time, holder of the ancient wisdoms.
"My child. To thine own self you must be true. For I walk this path
with you always.
Even when you don't see or feel me I am here.
Trust and believe.
For then the world of magic and of man will be as one".
The mighty dragon then left my side. Concealed within the mists.

)O(

I look around and what do I see?

I look around myself and what do I see?
A woodland glade with no one there but only you and me.
I listen very carefully to any sound I hear, a gentle stepping footfall
is coming very near.
Through the dancing sunbeams and coming into view, Is a
majestic magical being, one of only a few.
A nudge upon my shoulder and the warmth of his breath.
I look into his soft brown eyes, and I know his name is Draeth.
He walks by my side but only for a while.
Knowing that he is here for me really makes me smile.
From the Isle of Avalon only his kind are born.
My beautiful and magical enchanted unicorn.

)O(

Whispers of the Seeker

Avalon awaits. She is not lost to those that seek her. She only asks for trust and honesty. She will teach you all you need to know. The journey will be long and the path hard. The mists are lifting for but a moment, It is your choice to step through.
You will find many blessings as you walk through the veil.

~

To follow within the footsteps of the Mother Goddess you just simply need to see her.
She lives within all our hearts and homes. She is within the hug of the child. The purr of the cat. She dwells within the dancing butterfly on the delicate flower.
She is not lost to those that do not seek, she is but a heartbeat away.

~

The energy of the Priestess holds the key to the realms. The power of the ancients. It is true and empowering. But you must hold the truths within your path, for only then can you walk with Avalon in your heart.

~

Avalon is but one step away through the mists. Do you wish to leave all you know behind you to embrace her?
For she cannot be honoured part time. You must breath her with every breath.
The truth will set you free, yet so many hide in disillusion. To walk among Avalon with the Sisters of the craft. If you cannot hold the

truth for yourself. You cannot hold it within magic.
To be secretive and dismissive with the priestess is to be
dishonest with yourself.

~

Avalon is rising. Her energy becoming stronger. She is walking
amongst the realm of man.
Embrace and honour her and give her the strength to empower us
as we walk our path in her name.

~

The Mother of Avalon asks you to be true to yourself. Do not
shroud yourself in lies and
deceit. No matter how painful. Only a true heart can lift the mists to
reveal the power and magic of Avalon.

~

The Priestess energy asks you to cleanse your soul. Look into the
corners of your life and clean them. Let go of what no longer
serves you. To walk within Avalon you need to be
free. To hold the power of Avalon you need to be healed. Begin
today with the small things you always put away till tomorrow.

~

Sisters. The great mother asks us to release the ties that hold us
from walking within Avalon with every step. We need to bring her

into this world of man. She is rising once more.
We need to awaken the ancient ways for all. Now is the time to
show others the path and embrace them as they find their way.

~

The gentle energy of Avalon calls through the mists. Will you listen
to the call? Carry her with every breath you take. Every step you
make. She waits to embrace you. Do not lose her
within humanity. Stand alone from others and hold your virtues
high at all times.

~

Awoke this morning to the sound of the magpies calling me home.
Do you know how Avalon calls you? Which familiar finds you to
call you through the mists? Listen and watch carefully
and you will learn that one awaits to walk your path with you.

~

Blessings as the mists reveal the sacred truths that you desire. To
walk through the mists you must be honest with yourself. Hold your
truths no matter what others say. For Avalon can only be found
when you unlock the soul with the key of truth.

~

The Great Mother has sent the rains today. Cleansing and
purifying. She always gives us what we need. So embrace and

honour what you have. For it is always enough for you to walk your path right now.

~

The mother priestess talks to us in many ways. Listen to her and find the way she talks to you. For me it is through birds and plants. It is always changing and I am always learning. Listen and you will hear her.

~

What magical tools do we need as priestess of Avalon? We need knowledge of the old ways. Alchemy of the elements and the Green Earth. Empowerment beyond measure. Knowledge and honour of the fae and Great Mother. Above all else connection that reaches through the mists.

~

Within nature lies the greatest magic. Look around you to see it. You have all you need to harness and create the power. To walk within Avalon is to honour this energy and to empower your being.

~

Walk your path with honour with every step you take for you walk with the name of Avalon in your heart. A priestess respects all before her and within her.
The teachings of Avalon are clear. Be true to yourself and honour all around you. For not to

do so is to dishonour the Great Mother herself.

~

Are you ready to question all you know? Your life? Your family? Your choices? For to enter Avalon you must be ready to look into the abyss. For only then will you honour the truth of the Great Mother within and around you. Walk through the pain to your bliss to walk the path to Avalon. To lift the mist you must embrace your power. Do not belittle all that you are. Only hold truth in your heart. You hold the sacred key of the Priestesses, but only by stepping out of ego will the veil of the Great Mother lift. Embrace who you know you are without compromise.

~

To walk within the realm of Avalon you must walk within the veil of the mists. To step out of the realm of man. Out of ego. To be truly free follow your heart. The path to Avalon will open, you just have to follow it with love and passion.

~

May you take the sacred symbol with honour and blessings. Keeping it within your heart and soul. Only those willing to walk the path of the Great mother in the name of Avalon may bare the gift of the crescent moon.

~

What are the truths you seek within the veil of Avalon? How do you feel your path wound you here within this place within this time?

Open the circle by getting to get to know the sisters within it.
Many blessings to all those who have stepped inside.

~

To walk the path to Avalon. To lift the mist. You must embrace
your power. Do not belittle all that you are. Only hold truth in
your heart. You hold the sacred key of the priestess, but only by
stepping out of ego will the veil of the Great Mother lift. Embrace
who you know you are without compromise.

~

To follow within the footsteps of the Mother Goddess you just
simply need to see her. She lives within all our hearts and homes.
She is within the hug of the child. The purr of the cat. She dwells
within the dancing butterfly on the delicate flower. She is not lost to
those that do not seek, she is but a heartbeat away.

~

As the Mists of Avalon part today. I find myself standing alone,
gazing at the mysteries of the lake. They run deep like the
emotions within my soul. My hands feel warm with the magic that
runs through them. I turn and walk through the enchanted land that
I live within. Filled with magical beings and the fae. The mists
descend once more and I find myself standing in this world with
Avalon but a distant memory. But forever knowing of the magic
that lives within me .
May the wise woman from Avalon grant you your insights. To help
you read the signs within your life. To empower and enrich your life

and soul. May the Merlin give you strength as you walk your path. To walk when you are weary. To turn the corner when you feel lost, and to face the dark when there is no light to guide you.

~

I call upon the beauty of the lady and the strength of the lord to walk by your side. Enchanting your world with magic and wisdom. May the fae bless you and the ancients embrace you.

~

I bring blessings today from the great mother. She asks that you sweep your life of negativities for the coming months ahead. It is time to let go of those things in life that holds you back, physically, mentally and emotionally. Go out today and find a fallen leaf. Write upon it what you wish to release. Call upon the energy of the Great Mother to be with you and release the leaf into the winds. Watch it as it moves out of your life. Enjoy the freedom that the Great Mother brings when you allow her to.

~

May the phoenix bring fire to your life raising the passion and energy within you. May the Unicorns purify your spirit. Bringing peace and magic to your world. May the dragon stand over you as ancient protector. In all that you do and hold dear. May you always walk your path with honesty and growth.

~

I come from the isle of Avalon. Bringing perfect love and perfect trust into your life. May the old ones watch over you. The ancients guide you. The wise ones bring you wisdom. Those that have walked this path before bring you peace and harmony.

~

From Avalon I bring with me balance from the earth, wisdom from the air, energy from the fire, emotions from the water, strength from the Goddess and protection from the God. Embrace these elements into your life and bring balance and harmony into your world.

~

May the serenity of the gentle earth find a place with you. The wisdom of the gods fall upon you. The gentle caress of the Great Mother touch your soul and your path open up before you with every step.

~

I long for the days of Avalon. A time of being at one with nature. Of herbal knowledge and lore as natural as the breath. The power within deep and powerful. To walk within the realms we no longer see. To be at one with the sisters of the craft. To walk amongst those who do not believe with my head held high. To be the sabbats and the moon and the sun. But wait. I can create my Avalon right here and right now, all that stops me is me. I choose to walk within Avalon with every step I walk. What do you chose to create today?

As the Great Mother weaves her winter savages at us. We must take heed from her ferocious winds and drenching rains. We must look after this green planet that we dwell upon. We often feel that we are in control of this sentient planet, but every now and again she rises up to remind us of her power. That she is a living being. That we are mere travelers upon her green belly. We must honour her, rejoice her and protect her. For when we take the time to do these simple things. We will have learnt to do these things for ourselves too. Enjoy the world around you.

~

May she who is of all things walk with you today. He of strength and of the hunt walk softly within your heart. May the balance of the green Earth and the Great Mother bring a peace within your heart. The warmth of the Great Father sky bless your soul, as it awakens from its winter slumber.

~

Witch (male or female) or warlock is a modern adaptation to distinguish between power and relevance within the circle. The only distinction is the Mother Goddess and father God. That we follow. The name tags are a human one. Not of the Priest or priestess, for they hold no knowledge of the gender battle within our world. They just are the embodiment of the divine.

~

Gender only exists within ego. In the true craft there is the Priestess who is the energy of the great mother and the Priest who is the energy of the Horned father. Their energy is within equal balance. There is no battle of power, for they know that one does not exist without the other. They walk within perfect harmony of one another. They honour the breath that each takes. The inhale of the mother becomes the exhale of the father. They live within their own realms honouring the divine within themselves. They have the strength of one another at all times but do not need to knowledge that strength as it is the unspoken bond between them. The gender correctness exists in modern witchcraft has always been taken out of context.

~

May your path be blessed as you walk its distance. The Great Mother shadow every step. The Father of the hunt brings strength to your heart. The Mother Priestess bring blessings to you in every way.

)O(

Whispers of the rising power

Energy Quicken

Energy quicken energy rise through the land and across the skies.
The craft of the wise and path of the old, keepers of the secrets the ancients told.
Come to me now in this time and place, as I welcome the great mother into this space.
The circle drawn far and wide to protect all those who step inside.
Energy quicken, energy rise our soul is bound by the sacred ties.
Priestess am I forever more, deep within me the wise woman lore.
Lord of the hunt and the queen of the night, I harness my power of the seers sight.
Energy quicken energy rise, upon my breath are the whispered sighs.
Given to me by the elements four, to open up the directions door.
Walk with me to the magical place, full of ritual, power and grace.
Energy quicken, energy rise through the land and across the skies.

)O(

Whispers of the Whisperer

Have you noticed recently how much love the green earth has for us? We often walk hurriedly without hearing or seeing her. Feeling that we are so important. That we are grand and wonderful. Have you listened to the lungs of the earth? Within the whispering trees? Have you looked upon the earth with the beauty of the flowers and butterflies? It takes nature so long to craft beauty in each feather that she places upon the tiny bird. But it takes us just a moment to destroy it. Be kind to yourself and love the nature around you.

~

Friends are like the stars from the skies. They bring a light into our life when we need it the most. Sometimes we don't always see them or have contact with them but knowing that they are always there brings magic even to the darkest skies. At time the clouds hide who they are. At other times the stars map out the most beautiful mosaic of knowledge and information for us to read. I feel thankful for the stars that are within my life.

~

To find a part of your soul in another is to hold a piece of a star within your hand. A gift that is precious and very special. To be honoured and loved by a soul that enters your life is to honour a contract that was carved many universes ago and is being fulfilled now. It may bring pain or learning. Love or wisdom. Grief or gain. But remember you are special and everyone who enters your life is there because of who you are and what you have asked them to bring into your journey.

Through the mists of time all will be revealed. Will you take the time to wait? Or will you walk on passing life's treasures by? Will you allow the fae to enchant the unseen to be seen? Will you draw upon the power of this ancient land? To enrich your world and your life. Only you are the holder of the answer. Only you can decide. The ancients walk by your side always. Do you feel and honour them? They bring gifts to you daily. Do you notice them? For when you do your path becomes blessed threefold. Illuminating and opening up before you're very eyes. Blessed be upon your journey today. May the Great Mother walk within your heart and the Great Father within your soul.

~

Take a breath and cleanse your soul. Be thankful for what you have in your life. It may be something small that seems so tiny. But when you give thanks it opens the door for more wealth and riches to flow into your world. Be thankful for the green earth. Be thankful for the small things and allow the larger things in.

~

As I walk along today with the gentle spring sun upon my back, I realise that I am blessed to be part of the cycle of the Great Mother. The birds flying overhead with twigs and treasure within their beaks, making ready for their cycle of life to begin. The cold of the frost reminds me that winters grip is still but a breath away, and able to consume us at any moment. The delicate flowers that have birthed through the earth remind me of the beauty that is on its way. The quickening of life flowing through my veins gives me the energy to become who I want to be.
The beauty that is within my life gives my heart a gentle reminder, that all is not lost even on the darkest day, the sun will always rise.

We step for but a moment upon this fragile Earth. Make every step matter.

~

To walk the path of healing is to honour the reflection in front of you. To embrace the emotions it invokes. Not to take a peep and run away to where you think you can hide. It takes great strength to see between the tears, and honest truth to voice the words that lie unspoken. By honouring the truth you honour the self. Allowing release and growth. Let us walk together. Standing side by side. Holding each other's hand when we need it the most.

~

To thine own self be true. Hold the truth that is within you in gentle honour. Nurture and caress it as a treasured gift from the ancient civilizations that have walked this earth before us. We are them. They are us. We are one. The vibrations are quickening. Ascend with virtue and grace.

~

Smile to a stranger and make them feel wanted. Give a complement to another and help them feel loved. Hug the nearest to you for no reason whatsoever. Tell someone I love you just because. May the magic return to you threefold.

~

May grace touch your soul today, enchanting everything you do and say? Bringing light to the darkest place, seeing beauty in a strangers face. May you feel the magic from the ancient time? Remembering what's yours is mine. For we are all one connected together. Let's bring peace to our lives, always and forever.

~

Our Journey may be long or it may be short. It may be filled with fun or sadness. It may be lonely or filled with friends and family. You may never understand why you are here. You may have known from an early age that you have an important role to play. But remember you journey is spun into the web of life itself and your journey will cross others path. You will have an effect on them as they will with you. Shine the light on your journey and it will become illuminated for you.

~

As you live your lives today. Be aware of the hidden messages that are littered throughout the day. What does the song of the bird bring to you? The smile from a stranger? A hug from a friend? The joy of walking your path embracing the lessons. Remember today is for living. Tomorrow will always wait.

~

In a world where anger has strength and pain seems to find a hold within our lives. We can make a difference with a smile, a kind word or act. Let's change the energy of our world. Lets us stop being individuals and become a realm of our own reality of love. Stop but for a moment and take a breath. Draw in the very life of the earth. Slow time down just for a while and see the unseen.

Hear the unheard. Feel the unfelt. Forget money and possessions and see the wealth of the Great Mother. For then you will have found your greatest riches.

~

Have you noticed recently how much love the green earth has for us? We often walk hurriedly without hearing or seeing her. Feeling that we are so important. That we are grand and wonderful. Have you listened to the lungs of the earth? Within the whispering trees. Have you looked upon the earth with the beauty of the flowers and butterflies? It takes nature so long to craft beauty in each feather that she places upon the tiny bird. But it takes us just a moment to destroy it. Be kind to yourself and love the nature around you.

~

Have love in your heart, warmth in your eyes, laughter in your soul and compassion for all and you will never be alone. For the fae and magic will enchant your life always.

~

Sometimes in our life we feel alone. As if we have no one. It can feel lonely and sad. Remember if we feel and see the beauty within ourselves we are never alone for we will always find each other.

~

When we walk through the shadows of our life we have to walk alone. We have to feel and embrace the pain and emotions that live within the shadow. When we find the strength and courage to move through it we become enriched beyond measure. We become illuminated and our light gives others the strength to walk through the shadows within their lives. I have walked the shadows many times my friend and will do so many more times to come. But for now I shine my light for all. Bringing strength and courage.

~

Stop for but a moment. Take your feet out of your shoes and place your bare feet upon the naked earth. Stand very still and quiet. Feel the warmth that lives beneath you. Allow the heartbeat of the earth to fill your being until both your hearts beat as one. Listen to the whisper within the trees and the love the earth has for us as her gift. Place a little of her beauty within your heart and share this gift with others within your smile.

~

We live for so long with anger and sorrow within our hearts. Often from our childhood or from adult hurts and pain. That we forget how unconditional love and joy can feel. Often we don't trust when we do experience love and are waiting for the pain to start. Never fully living in the moment. Always with a foot in the past and one in the future. If you find yourself reading this today. Stop for but a moment and close your eyes. Breathe. Connect with a moment of pure joy and bliss, no matter how tiny and draw it into your soul. Allow your body to feel the love and place it deeply within your heart. Allow the journey of unconditional love for yourself to begin. Love is blind. It falls upon the unexpected. It is unconditional. It doesn't judge or humiliate. It nurtures and gives hope. It brings a belonging and warmth. It brings friendship to the lonely and creation to life. Only when we take it and place it within the human does it become a destroyer and a prize. Unreachable for some and a weapon to others. Let love become its pure energy once more and not control it. Set the love within you free without fear.

~

Every day when I open my eyes, I feel thankful for the people that will come into my life today, for what they will teach me. The good , the bad and sometimes the sad. I am glad that I feel sorrow and joy. Pain and comfort. For this makes me alive. It moves me forward on my life lessons. It makes me count my blessings whatever they are. Even in my darkest hour, I trust I will see the light again.

~

May today bring you happiness and joy. Even if it is the smallest glimpse, hold it within your heart, and share it. For when you do it grows and spreads through your body. Healing and balancing, clearing away the negativity and hurts. Smile for no reason. Hug just because. And love like for the first time.

~

Sometimes we feel low for no reason. Like everything that can go wrong will go wrong. It feels like we are alone that no one understands. Everyone is wrapped up in their lives and has no time for yours. Try and remember that in your darkest hour the light can shine brightest. It will pass. Just reach out and ask for a hug. Or just someone to talk too. We are only alone if we choose to be. Connect and you will find what your looking for.

~

I awoke today to the sound of magpies chatting outside my window. And the birds singing in the trees and my cats asking for breakfast in the usual way. It find it so inspiring how nature finds its way to us if we allow it. It will come and find you if you just listen and be still. Sometimes we move so fast within in our lives that we lose our connection. Go and find your connection today. It's the best tonic and medicine in the world and for free.

~

Take a breath and cleanse your soul. Be thankful for what you have in your life. It may be something small that seems so tiny. But when you give thanks it opens the door for more wealth and riches to flow into your world. Be thankful for the green earth. Be thankful for the small things and allow the greater things in.

~

Blessings to you from the green earth and the blue skies. Take your strength from the great mother as she stands by you today. And your wisdom from the great father as he stands behind you it feels as there is a turning point ahead that we must all take as individuals but will affect us all as a group. Embrace the journey as all is always as it should be.

Everything is for a reason. The lesson is to be still long enough to be patient to see the lesson and understand the reason. Be still just for a moment today and find the reason for the lessons within your life. For then you will grow and travel your journey with clarity and understanding.

~

There is no greater lesson in life than that of the family. From our tribal and clan beginnings. We have been drawn together in soul families. They may be lessons of heartache and pain. Love and pure joy. Death or the removal of innocence. But we chose our

family lesson and journey. However your family is .Whether its strong or weak. Broken or close. Be thankful for what you have learnt. Break the cycle if you don't like what you find and create a new cycle with your own.

~

Sometimes we walk around consumed by our own lives. The troubles and woes that make us regroup and look deeply at ourselves. Some however walk around consumed by the human journey and unable to reach and connect with their soul. If we take but a moment on our spiritual journey full of lessons and layers we can reach out to those who seem lost. A simple smile. A word of the wise. A listening ear. Or just a hug can make the difference between a soul walking in darkness and a being transforming into a brilliant light.

~

It is good to let others see a side of us that we hold deep within. Just to let go and be who we hide from externally. Have some fun.

Go dancing. Sing at the top of your voice. Let others stand back and watch in awe a side of you they have never seen. Let people say. I never knew. How will you feed your soul today? Feed your soul with joy and wonder.

~

If we face our fears. The fears disappear. If we fail to look it grows into something we cannot face. Our fear is just the unknown or someone else's fear. Projected onto us. We only get given what we can face and deal with. We have the strength. We just have to draw upon it. We are here to learn, not to be hurt, in pain, sad or alone. If we face those things and accept our lessons then our journey can be free of the fears and pain. It's just up to us how quickly we look for the lessons.

~

We can get pulled into the energy of others lives. Their troubles, Pain, despair, loneliness, Illness, stress and anxiety. Sometimes Happiness, joy and celebration. We need to touch on all these emotions to be free and alive. Don't try and wear them for others. They must do it for themselves. But be the solid oak behind them that will support and protect them on their journey. Equally when you find yourself in a similar place allow those you have helped to be your oak. So you to can feel and learn your lessons and grow.

~

Lessons in life can be the hardest part within our journey. If we honestly embrace that lesson with our body and soul. We can move forward so quickly. But if we find ourselves locked within the fear we halt. Stand still. Rooted to the spot. Like a rabbit within the headlights. Too frightened to run. Too frightened to stand and fight. So we give up, becoming the lesson. Consumed by the energy and the victim within us. So today look at your lessons. Choose to learn and transform your life.

~

Sometimes we lose more than we can bear. A life , a soul of those who we care. It leaves us feeling so alone. An empty space within our home. Our heart feels like it will never recover. We will never find such love in another. Time will heal, that empty space. Once it has healed with love and grace. Just know that you are loved in every way. And just get yourself through today. The soul you lost will walk with you. Beside your side always true. They have gone only from the physical plane. Together in spirit you will be again. Enjoy the world around you.

~

To stand alone takes bravery and strength, to stand together takes grace and love. At times we feel week and alone, as if at every turn we hit a wall, a blockage upon our path. Right within that moment you have the choice. Alone or with others? It is your choice. You are not dealt your response. You choose it, so choose willingly. Embrace your choice. If it is to be alone. Be strong and true to your choices. If it is with others, allow them in. Trust and rely upon them. For then you will no longer be weak or lonely.

We tend to forget the reason for our being. That we choose to journey upon this mighty planet. We often need to remind ourselves that we are spiritual beings on a human experience. But we are not human. We are so much more. We are all capable of great things. No one is more gifted or connected than the other. Just tap inside of yourself. Tune into that mighty spirit that dwells within. Connect to the higher consciousness of the soul. You are never alone. You are part of something wondrous and expansive. Just be still long enough to feel and hear it.

~

Do you listen to your heart? Do you take heed of your soul? Or do you constantly put others needs before your own? If you asked yourself what you really want. What would be your answer? Do it now, right now. And listen to the first thing you hear. Why do we constantly lie to ourselves and put others first? Because humanity has conditioned us to do so for such a long time. Embrace the new energy around us. Be selfish and put yourself first. For then you will truly be able to help others. As your soul grows to the size it should always be. Enjoy the world around you.

~

You can cut an apple open and count the seeds within, but only the Great Mother knows how many apples are within the seed. This is a wonderful symbol of our journey upon this great earth. For we may feel we have control within our lives. But we never know what is awaiting for us until it grows and blossoms. Enjoy every step and enjoy the fruits that await for you along your path.

Blessed be to those who read my words and help me to walk my path. Blessed be to those friends who hearts are touched and opened to the love that I send with each message. Blessed be for the path you have chosen to walk, for no matter how hard, lonely or bleak you may find it at times, it is your path and one to be walked with honour and honesty. I honour the divine light within your soul and wish for you blessings as you travel your journey and find the light that I already see deep within you.

~

To live a life with sadness and pain. Is to live a life in vain. To embrace your woes your enemies and foes is to live your truth. Don't live empty and sad .

~

The love that is shown to us when we need and ask for it can be overwhelming. It only takes a moment to tell someone how much they mean to you. The effect they have had upon your life. But it can mean so much to the person you are telling. So you mean a great deal to me dear friend. And have enriched my life beyond belief. So thank you for being part of my wonderful journey upon this beautiful Earth.

~

On our journey you just have to trust , that all is as it should be right now. It is only when the ego decides that we shouldn't be where we find ourselves that we find life a struggle. Are you are trying to swim against the current? Just let yourself be washed away with the flow of life, and oddly enough you will get what you need.

I live my life that if things are to hard to gain, then they are not mine to have, what comes with ease is what is meant to be. Are you where you are meant to be ? Maybe you need to change direction. What comes easily to you is where you are meant to go now be still. Feel it. Breathe it. Be it. Embrace the surrender. Own it and make it yours. It does not belong to anyone else. Only look for the full surrender within. For that is where you will find it. Allow others to journey their own path. You must travel yours alone right now, do not hold energy for anyone else but yourself. Go forth and grow into who you know you already are, but to afraid to see .

~

It saddens me when folk lose their light and lose their soul within the night. When they only speak out of fear and fright. If only we could be one light, from the universe and the stars such a divine love could be ours. Filled with the unicorn and the fae, dragons and wisdom. At one we would be in a magical kingdom. Lets show them the way , you and I . Let's show their souls how to fly. Hold my hand so very tight and shine our beautiful rainbow light.

~

To be is to find an answer. One that feels so right. To walk a path of virtue and hold an inner light. To shine upon the darkest hour showing the lost the way. And to be silent but always have your say. To hold a power greater than man deep inside your heart. To look within the mirror is the very start.

~

To BE for but a moment is to open up your soul. A gateway to the energies that help us reach our goal. To notice all around us, is to be at peace with all. If you listen very carefully you will hear the ancient call. Embrace the signs of nature, for they hold the hidden keys. Enjoy the world around you with love.

~

You need to learn to JUST BE. Stop searching. You embrace every new thing that passes you, trying to make it your own. Just listen to your soul. It talks clearly , but you don't listen. Just pause and just be .You just have to trust , that all is as it should be right now. It is only when the ego decides that we shouldn't be where we find ourselves that we find life a struggle. Are you are trying to swim against the current, just let yourself be washed away with the flow of life, and oddly enough you will get what you need. I life my life that if things are to hard to gain, then they are not mine to have, what domes with ease is what is meant to be. You can be washed away in surrender or in victim.. you need to decide which is you. Now be still. Feel it. Breathe it. Be it. Embrace the surrender. Own it and make it yours. It does not belong to anyone else. Only look for the full surrender within. For that is where you will find it. Allow others to journey their own path. You must travel yours alone right now, do not hold energy for anyone else but yourself. Go forth and grow into who you know you already are, but to afraid to see .

~

To be is to find an answer. One that feels so right. To walk a path of virtue and hold an inner light. To shine upon the darkest hour showing the lost the way. And to be silent but always have your say. To hold a power greater than man deep inside your heart. To look within the mirror is the very start.

~

Inside your heart is the cosmic truth to your soul. The blueprint of divinity. It is your choice to attune to the rhythm of the heart beat to listen to its sacred message

~

To hold a truth within your hand, is to be touched by the great mother. Only truth and Innocence lives within the realms of nature. Lies, deceit and horror only lies within the realm of man. Open your heart to the Hunter and lady, to embrace the energy of the land, and place it within your heart. It is the key to Avalon and the land of the fae

~

When you shine brightly. Do not allow yourself to be dimmed by those who only shine in the dark. To shine in the bright light of the universe is to shine brightest of all.

~

To look into the abyss and face the fear, takes strength beyond measure. We all have the strength within us. Fear is not within our soul's blueprint, it is a human emotion. Do you choose the human fear to lock you into the human ego, or do you choose to embrace the abyss and unlock the diva's of your soul

~

Focus on those that bring you joy within your heart and soul and release the ones who wish to bring darkness. You know who you are. Your energy lights the way before you. Hold it aloft when those who are too afraid to look in the mirror stand before you, and blind them with the illuminated energy of love you hold.

~

From the stars you and me. Our greatest lesson is to just BE.
To hold the energy of man and the land. As we lead each other by the hand.
Our consciousness together as one. Drawn together from when time begun.
Priestess warrior's from the Universe above. Sent to bring harmony and love.
As we transition to the energies anew. Our aura coloured with the Indigo hue.
The new world is awaiting right now. To create it is our honoured vow

~

For all that you are. All you can ever be. For all you have seen , and all you will see. For the path you have travelled, and the path yet to come. Believe in yourself and the magic is done.

~

To learn the lessons that are bestowed upon us. To at times walk within shadow. But at all times to walk with the ancients openly as we listen to their guidance.. Be it the bird that flies past us. The raindrop within the spiders web .The unique flower that opens at spring. Embrace all as you learn and grow and become the Priestess of Avalon.

~

To walk the path of healing is to honour the reflection in front of you. To embrace the emotions it invokes. Not to take a peep and run away to where you think you can hide. It takes great strength to see between the tears, and honest truth to voice the words that lie unspoken. By honouring the truth you honour the self. Allowing release and growth. Let us walk together. Standing side by side. Holding each other's hand and helping us to see the unseen.

~

Whispers of the Moon

Moon Maiden

Moon Maiden whisper to me, of all the things you know I can be.

Moon Mother nurture me deep, as I give you my tender soul to keep.

Moon Crone the wise old sage, give me your wisdom as I age.

The triple Goddess in your moon of full, how my soul feels your sacred pull.

As you shine upon me on this moonlit night, I will honour your teachings within my rite.

Moon Goddess you live within me, my soul is yours for eternity

)O(

The Lady of the Moon

The lady of the Moon breathes life into her fullness as we reach
the time of the Dyad moon. She lifts the veil to Avalon for those
who have taken the oath of her path.
The lovers, become paired in their union of the gentle moon and
the pulsating sun.
In ritualistic chant the priestess call upon the Great Mother and
the Green Man to fortify the union of the Earth and sky.
Incense fills the air with smoke and sent that releases the soul and
opens the doors of the realms. The sun holds itself within the sky
and the moon rises in harmony to the rhythmic chant of the elders.

The eclipsing moon embraces the sun as a mother does a child.
The energy of the ancients embraced by the priestess as she turns
her face up to the sky. The mists spiraling at her feet. The energies
within her hands. Her head full of the ancient knowledge and
wisdom that has flowed within her body since her time of birth.

All she is and all she knows is right here and right now, within this
time and space.
A priestess of the old ways. Daughter of old. She weaves her
magic into the night.

)O(

May you be blessed

May you be blessed threefold upon this May full moon. Moon of
many names. Hare moon. Sap moon . Flower moon.
As she releases her energy upon those that welcome it, may you
find balance, power and strength as she illuminates your path.
Many blessings.

)O(

Many Blessings to you at the time of the April seed moon

Many blessings to you at the time of the April seed moon. The time of planting your desires deep within the belly of the Great Mother. Whilst feeding and nurturing her, she will in turn nurture your wants and needs. The moon seems so powerful right now. Shrouded in mystical enchantment. As I gazed upon her last night, it was as if she had become a beacon for us. One to guide and follow, as she always is but more intense. There are shifts afoot, the soul is awakening and the ancients are rising. Enjoy your moon, may she bless your path as she illuminates your journey upon it.

)O(

Distant Moon

Distant moon rising in the skies, I look upon you with ancient eyes.
Full of magic, enchantment and rite, I walk the path this star filled
night.
As you shine behind the mist, the ancient chants I cannot resist.
The song of the maiden, mother and crone, lives in my breath, my
blood and bones.
As my sisters gather in sacred space, we will honour the wise ones
within this place.
In this time and upon the hour, Avalon will rise with her Priestess
power.

)O(

Darksome moon shining bright

Darksome moon shining bright above the earth. We celebrate
tonight with reverence and mirth.
Witches stand together or alone, souls connected by blood and by
bone.
Draw the energy deep within, as the moon celebrations now begin.
Cast a spell and make it so, but tell not a soul not one can know.
Enjoy dear sisters one and all, when you hear the ancient witches
call.

)O(

Under the stars of the Moonlit sky

Under the stars of the moonlit sky, that has watched me so many
times.
I stand within the gentle moonlight and connect to the ties that
bind.
With arms outstretched and opened wide, I embrace all that I can
be.
For within my soul from the ancients and olds, the Great Mother
always sees me.

The gracious moon Mother recognises me as the daughter of her
kin.
Through the mists and within Avalon I know my journey did begin.
I stand here now under the July Full Moon on my path with honour
and lore.
Each time I look upon her it is as if it's for the first time and not
ever once before.

Hay moon of the ancient times I beckon thee to me.
Of all the things I have not been, I release now willingly.
As the time of Lughnasagd turns the wheel of the sacred lands
once more.
I shall harvest what I have sown with thanks from deep within my
core.

I energise my path and soul by the whisper of your moonlight.
As I celebrate with my sisters within the Avalon Isle tonight.
Hail thee Great mother Goddess ,allow me to be all I can be.
With your loving guidance and watchful eye evermore shall I be
free.

)O(

I open my eyes and what do I see ?

I open my eyes and what do I see ? The gentle glowing moon shining down at me. She glows so brightly on this dark winters night. My room is awash with the crescent moonlight. She lies on her back as she starts to wane. But her energy still flows through the window pane. The stars gather round her, for she is never alone. As she brings me the messages from my forgotten home. She unlocks the priestess that dwells within me. Just embrace her now and you to will see. I now face the day refreshed and anew. Now she waits to bring her gifts to you. Blessed be my friend.

)O(

The dark of the moon rises within me

The dark of the moon rises within me, and the shadows come as I embrace thee.

For within the dark is the balance of my power, I honour and embrace within this hour.

To work in the craft, to stand in the light I must hold the energy's of the night.

The Crone, the wise the ancient and old, lives in the dark and her I enfold.

The enrapture of the power upon this night the dark of the moon hidden from sight.

The energies rise from the Avalonion mists I hear her call and do not resist.

My sisters I find within the dark of the moon, My return has come not a moment to soon.

For I feel her now pulsating through me. Forever more a Priestess I be.

The dark of the moon shines upon me now, How I embrace the great Crone in humbled bow.

)O(

In the darkness of the deepest shining moonlight

In the darkness of the deepest shining moonlight, Silvery shadows
can be seen just out of sight.
In the moss filled glade where magic resides, the realm of the Fae
lives where it hides.
You can call to them on the whisper of the breath, in the moments
calm that seems like death.
The key to the realm is given to you, and through the door you
now pass through.

An enchanted sight beholds your gaze, As your soul is transfixed
in silent amaze.
Of all the tales you have been told before, here all becomes true ,
but so much more.
The sprites are abundant in their truest guise , flitting between
Earth, the stars and the sky.
The Pixies are gathering all that shines, and placing them lovingly
on their wildwood shrines.

The Gnomes of the Earth tender their wondrous plants, from the
tiniest bud to the towering branch.
With a gentle step and a tender eye, The Unicorn stands between
the Earth and the sky.
Majestic in sight and old to the wise, The dragon descends from
the star studded skies.
Within this place you are all you can be, Just close your eyes and
you too will see.

)O(

The moon rises upon distant sky,

The moon rises upon distant sky, the reflection is seen within the
Priestesses eye.

The October moon the one of blood, of the full harvest, and of the
flood.

The fire is lit upon the night, and the moon is honoured within her
rite.

From ancient times to the days of now, many have stood in time
honoured vow.

As the Earth withdraws into her womb, restoring her energy for her
to bloom.

The Moons gentle rays illuminate all, as the energies rise and to
the Priestesses call.

Energy quicken in this sacred space, as Avalon rises to her rightful
place.

Blessings upon you at this moon of full, may you honour the
wisdom of the wise ones pull.

)O(

As I stand at my window

As I stand at my window, and gaze upon the dancing trees, I see
the moon hidden behind the moving leaves.
Her aura is astonishing bright for all to see, and as I fall asleep
tonight I know she will shine upon me.
The magic is within her power covered within a veil of mist. It
streams from the heavens into my gentle fist.
My power and my strength, my key to Avalon, I see the mists part
and a boat I stand upon.
The moon she shines bright tonight and Avalon I now see.
Guided by the magic and the white ancient light. home I now be.

)O(

Wolf moon

The dark has weighed heavy within the night, and the wheel
ground slowly from Mid Winter to the light.
My energy slowed as I turned within , but now with this moon new
life begins. The moon of wolf is on the prowl, as the energy rises
you will feel its howl. Time to protect all you hold dear, draw your
circle and your loved ones near.

The energy quickens as the land renews, only Avalon stands
before my view.
I feel the Lady whisper to me once more, as she stands within the
mist like often before.
I hail my sisters upon this full moon night as we connect together
in ritual and rite.
Time to begin the cycle once more, the rhythm of life within my
core.

May the full moon rise within your sky, as you hold Avalon within
the mist of your eye.
Full moon blessings to you my friends, As you make true your
energy will bend.
The night of magic and power of rite, is held in the Priest and
Priestesses sight.
May your rituals be blessed by the ancients of old, as you embrace
the wolf moon of cold.

)O(

Moon of Ice

I embrace the February moon of ice, I welcome her once and bless
her twice.
As she melts the Earth down below, the awakening energies begin
to flow.
The time of wait is coming to its end, quickening energies the lady
does send.

The harshness of winter behind us once more, the earth is
warming within her core.
The life giving energy is within the moon, as we embrace her
fullness our soul does attune.
Our time of retreat, pausing and wait, as our energy wakens and
begins to pulsate.

The moon awakens the promise within, as the Mother moves from
Winter to Spring.
She rises so bright within the sky, and the magic is held within the
Priestesses eye.
Time for life to begin anew, embrace her now as she courses
through you.

)O(

Hare Moon

The hare is with the moon as he stares into the sky, how he longs
to look deep within her eye.
He sits and waits upon the breath of the Earth, and he feels the
energy of the ladies gentle birth.
The moon she hangs low within the sky, as the moon gazing hare
lets out a heavy sigh.

How he wishes he was within the stars, he would leap on the
planets from Jupiter to Mars.
The moon she wept as she saw his love, and she gently came
down from the heavens above.
She embraced him with the kiss of the Mother and of the Maiden,
the Crone and also the lover.

His heart skipped a beat as she held him so tight, and she carried
him tenderly into the night.
The Moon and the hare bring their love to the Earth, as the
Equinox energy brings about rebirth.
Light and dark are of equal length yet the light is growing stronger,
the days of the dark we are living within no longer.

The March moon of full holds the hare within its glow, as she
releases the last of the harsh winter's snow.
With the Equinox not far behind, new life and fertility is within the
hare's mind.
As the priestess shape shifts into this magical beast, she
welcomes him always at her magical feasts.

)O(

Moon Blessings

Blessings to you on the August moon of full. The wort moon. A time to preserve what is yours for the coming dark days of winter. May the goddess bless you with her wisdom, and the god bless you with strength as the wheel turns towards the darker days.

~

Blessings today for the October Harvest blood Moon. A time to remember those who have passed from this world. Making an offering to them for all they have taught you. Take the opportunity of the harvest moon to harvest all those little things that you have put off. This is the last chance to reap the bounty that you have lovingly grown. So enjoy them or let them go.

~

Blessings to you at this time of the November Snow moon. A time to rid yourself of negative thoughts and vibrations. To make way for the new wheel that awaits you for the coming year. For you cannot move forward if you are tied to the past.

~

May the Barley moon of September shine bright upon you tonight. Allowing you to give thanks for all the old ones have given you. May the full moon bless you with your needs and wants. As you receive the bounty from the God and Goddess within your life that you richly deserve.

Many blessings to you at this time of the milk moon. Moon of the winds. A time of asking the old ones for help with planning your future. As the moon shines upon you tonight may you be blessed by the goddess as she awakens your soul. Taking you into her arms as she readies you for the equinox. Have an enchanted moon.

~

As the moon of March illuminates your soul tonight, allow yourself to begin to fulfill your dreams. Release the Hare of the moon into your life, and bring about the energy to weave your web of Transformation. Full moon blessings.

~

Many blessings to you at this time of the milk moon. Moon of the winds. A time of asking the old ones for help with planning your future. As the moon shines upon you tonight may you be blessed by the goddess as she awakens your soul. Taking you into her arms as she readies you for the equinox. Have an enchanted moon.

)O(

Contact

From the Whispers of Avalon

Website www.fromthewhispersofavalon.co.uk
Email whispersofavalon@btinternet.com
Facebook www.facebook.com/whispersofavalon
Radio www.oneworldradio.org.uk

~

Phiona also teaches the 9 veils of the Avalon Sisterhood for more information:

Sisters of the Mists. Priestesshood of the Ancient ways

Website www.sistersofthemists.co.uk
Email sistersofthemists@btinternet.com
Facebook www.facebook.com/sistersofthemists

~

Phiona can also be booked for private healing and reading sessions for more information:

Avalon Whispering. Healing of the ancient ways

Website www.avalonwhispering.co.uk
Email avalonwhispering@btinternet.com

~

Notes